180 PRAYERS FOR A MAN OF GOD

180 PRAYERS FOR A MAN OF GOD

BARBOUR
PUBLISHING

Member of the
Evangelical Christian
Publishers Association

Printed in China.

INTRODUCTION

The 180 thought-provoking prayers on these pages are written especially for men from a man's perspective. The prayers appeal to the emotions as well as the intellect and draw the heart and mind closer to God by expressing love, contrition, thanksgiving, and supplication.

The text addresses topics of particular interest to men such as morality, integrity, and faithfulness. The book is designed for use during private devotions, but it can be a springboard for discussion in a Sunday school class or a study group.

All prayers begin with a scripture quotation. The verses are compelling reminders that God promises to bless those who speak to Him with humility and live faithfully. Scripture, inspired by God, was given so "That the man of God may be perfect, thoroughly furnished unto all good works" (2 Timothy 3:17).

HOMECOMING

*Keep yourselves in the love of God,
looking for the mercy of our Lord
Jesus Christ unto eternal life.*
JUDE 1:21

Heavenly Father, as the airplane I was in descended through the clouds to land, the ride became bumpy. The plane shook as the lashing rain buffeted it. But after we dipped below the clouds and touched down, the setting sun illuminated everything with a warm glow. At the gate, my family welcomed me home.

Lord, like that airplane flight, a few bumps have reminded me of how blessed the rest of my life has been. When I arrive at my final destination, I will be illuminated by Your light. Those who have gone before me will be there, welcoming me home. Lord, help me prepare for living in a home not made with human hands.

TOUCHING JESUS

Finally, be ye all of one mind,
having compassion one of another,
love as brethren, be pitiful, be courteous.
1 Peter 3:8

Lord Jesus, I read in the Bible that by coming to the rescue of those who are hungry and thirsty, I am touching You. Help me never accept pain and suffering as a natural condition. Guide me to show the compassion that You had when You healed the sick and fed the hungry multitudes. Help me put sympathy into action for those who suffer.

Heavenly Father, I thank You for Your watchful eye upon me. Guide me to bring a concrete expression of love to others who have a physical or emotional crisis. Provide me with the wisdom and the means to relieve the suffering of others.

A PERSONAL PRAYER

And this is life eternal, that they might know
thee the only true God, and Jesus
Christ, whom thou hast sent.
Jᴏʜɴ 17:3

Heavenly Father, in this prayer I want to speak to You about myself. I pray that it is not a selfish prayer, for my ultimate goal is to be right with You. Please make a way for me to avoid sin and help me to accept Your forgiveness when I do sin. I long to be right with You. Direct my steps to always be in the path of righteousness.

Father, help me recognize the work You have given me to do, and assist me as I try to glorify You. Stamp Your name on my heart so that I may live eternally in Your presence.

LIGHTING THE DARK

The night is far spent, the day is at hand:
let us therefore cast off the works of darkness,
and let us put on the armour of light.
Romans 13:12

Heavenly Father, this valley that I walk in has two different aspects depending on the angle of the sun. In the evening, the shadow of a hill casts the valley into deep gloom. But in the early hours of the day, the valley is bright because it faces the morning sun.

Father, what a difference the sun makes in the natural world, and what a difference when I see my life with the light You provide! When I walk through dark passages in my life, I pray that my eyes will be opened to the illumination that You provide. Give me a positive outlook to overcome the dreary times. Keep me in the light of Your blessings.

WHAT UPSETS YOU?

*For the flesh lusteth against the Spirit, and the
Spirit against the flesh: and these are contrary
the one to the other: so that ye cannot
do the things that ye would.*
GALATIANS 5:17

Heavenly Counselor, I encounter many problems
each day. Sometimes they arise from the simple
struggles of daily life, like a car with a dead battery
or a home with a faulty hot water tank. Keep me
from becoming upset because of inanimate objects.
Sometimes I have conflicts with people whose business objectives are different from mine. Help me
refuse to act improperly in daily give-and-take with
others. I too struggle with my own limitations, like
forgetfulness. May I never become frustrated by my
lack of proficiency.

Father, one conflict I especially want to avoid is
one with the Holy Spirit. May I never work against
Your purposes.

OPEN-DOOR POLICY

Thou shalt guide me with thy counsel,
and afterward receive me to glory.
Psalm 73:24

Lord, I once had a supervisor who had an open-door policy. Whenever I was torn about the best course of action to solve a problem, I would spend a few minutes talking with him. Sometimes he would suggest an option; sometimes he would caution me against an option.

I am thankful, Father, that You have an open-door policy. I can talk to You day or night about the things that trouble me. It is a comfort to know that You are there to listen. I know that You will make clear to me the correct decision.

SETTING A COURSE

*What man is he that feareth the L*ORD*?*
him shall he teach in the way
that he shall choose.
PSALM 25:12

Lord, I watch the rain and see two raindrops fall only inches apart: One flows to the right, the other flows to the left.

Unlike the raindrops, I have the liberty to choose which direction my life flows. Heavenly Father, keep me from making careless judgments that can develop into frightful consequences. Guide me to choices that lead away from the darkness of sin and into the light of righteousness. Give me Your wisdom as I make choices. I pray that my decisions are based on the values instilled in me by studying Your Word.

TRUST IN THE LORD

*Trust in the LORD with all thine heart;
and lean not unto thine own understanding.*
PROVERBS 3:5

Father, on the way to work I saw a high-rise office building under construction. At dizzying heights, the workers appeared unconcerned as they walked on narrow ribbons of steel. That is something I could not do. Yet, set the same steel beam a few inches above the ground, and I could walk across it without concern.

Father, when I am apprehensive about tasks that need to be done, remind me that Your protective hand is under me. I pray that I will learn to step out in faith, secure in the knowledge that You are there for me.

OVERCOMING FEAR

Watch ye, stand fast in the faith,
quit you like men, be strong.
1 Corinthians 16:13

Father, I pray that I can overcome fears that hinder me from following in Your footsteps. Fear makes me a liar: I excuse myself by claiming that I don't know how or that I'm not ready. Fear makes me a pretender: I can be fainthearted or hesitant, and I call it patience.

Regardless of the nature of my anxiety, I must press ahead. Lord, may I embrace Your Word in order to drive out irrational concerns that trouble my heart. I pray that I will not allow fear to paralyze me.

GIVING WISE COUNSEL

Behold, God exalteth by his power:
who teacheth like him?
JOB 36:22

Lord, the opportunity to shape other lives is both a blessing and an awesome responsibility. Show me how to admonish, correct, and inspire those who come to me for guidance, whether it be at work, at church, or in the community. Help me build relationships founded on trust.

Lord, no one teaches like You; regardless of the circumstances, I pray I will ground my advice in Your Word. Give me the dedication and calm self-assurance to help the people I am mentoring realize higher objectives for their lives. I pray that they will have the conviction to remain on course when I am no longer guiding them.

LOVING UNITY

Can two walk together,
except they be agreed?
Amos 3:3

Dear Lord, I am disheartened to encounter disagreement among those who profess to believe in You: fractured denominations, split congregations, and individuals who no longer speak to one another. We should be pulling together. Unfortunately, I confess that because of my own obstinacy, I have contributed to the lack of harmony.

Lord, I pray that I will be more agreeable, that I will not be arrogant or unreasonable. Guide me to choose the right words that will lead to a better walk with You and with my brothers and sisters in Christ. Remind me that even if I am right, I can still be wrong if my comments are not wrapped in love.

INTELLECTUAL APPEAL

*The simple believeth every word: but the
prudent man looketh well to his going.*
PROVERBS 14:15

Lord, every day my eyes and ears are assailed by those who want to bend my will to their purposes. Testimonies from famous personalities, glittering television advertisements, and half-truths of insincere politicians are all trying to muddle my reasoning so I cannot distinguish between truth and lies. They want me to listen and not ask questions.

Father, help me use the abilities You have given me to carefully evaluate the claims of those who try to influence me. I appreciate that You appeal to my intellect as well as my emotions. You tell me to work out my own salvation and try the spirits to see if they are from You. Give me discernment in spiritual and everyday matters.

PURPOSE

*And we know that all things work together for
good to them that love God, to them who
are the called according to his purpose.*
ROMANS 8:28

Yesterday, Father, I watched a child put together a puzzle. At first, the pieces were all mixed together. One by one, the child fitted the pieces together to form the complete picture.

Lord, before I gave my heart to You and began to seek Your will, my life was a confused collection of parts. But as I develop a personal relationship with You, I begin to see a clearer image of what You have in store for me. Although my future is not yet fully revealed, I will gladly put the disarrayed components of my life into Your hands to complete the picture.

THE END

For God so loved the world, that he gave his only begotten Son, that whosoever believeth in him should not perish, but have everlasting life.
JOHN 3:16

Father, I avoid reading movie or book reviews that go into too much detail about the plot. I enjoy the suspense of waiting to learn how the story unfolds. The ending may be happy or it may have a twist, but I want to be surprised by it.

However, in my own life I want to know the final result. Thank You, Lord, for telling me the outcome. You have promised that if I seek You, I will find You. Jesus has already paid the penalty for my sins. A faithful life assures me that I will have an eternal home with You.

THE PICTURE JESUS SEES

According as he hath chosen us in him before the foundation of the world, that we should be holy and without blame before him in love.
EPHESIANS 1:4

Dear Lord, with an auto-everything digital camera, even I can take pictures. But I have found that snapping the shutter does not guarantee a good photo. I've learned to aim the camera to cut out distracting elements such as road signs, to avoid trees growing out of heads, and to keep power lines from cutting across a scenic view. Some times I have to use a flash to illuminate a dark subject.

Jesus, in Your honored position of viewing earth from heaven, what image of my life do You see? Remove all distracting elements from my Christian character. Illuminate me with Your love, and frame me in Your Word. I pray You will compose my life so it presents a pleasing picture to others—and to You.

ENTER WITH THANKSGIVING

And God said unto Moses, I Am That I Am: and he said, Thus shalt thou say unto the children of Israel, I Am hath sent me unto you.
Exodus 3:14

Father, I pray that I may always enter Your presence in the proper way. I resolve to acknowledge with thanksgiving what You have done for me. You are merciful, long-suffering, and mindful of me. I praise You for the blessings that flow from You.

Lord, I come before You with humility. I bow before You, the Creator who called everything into existence. I bow in awe of You as I realize You are the I Am, the eternal presence that has spanned the ages. I humbly cry to You as my provider and deliverer.

AN EFFECTIVE TEACHER

For I have given you an example,
that ye should do as I have done to you.
JOHN 13:15

"Model the ideal behavior," a supervisor told me when I was taking a class to train others. "Show examples of the skill you want to transfer to the other employees, and give them guided practice."

Heavenly Father, I appreciate reading about the life of Your Son and seeing how He taught the world about Your love through His example and teachings. He portrayed compassion by healing the sick and feeding the multitudes. He expressed the depth of Your forgiveness by giving His life for my sins. Lord, help me communicate Your teachings by my example.

HAPPY IN THE LORD

*Happy is that people, that is in such a case: yea, happy is that people, whose God is the L*ORD.
PSALM 144:15

Lord, as I look up to heaven, I am overwhelmed with a spirit of happiness. I delight in knowing You as the Creator of this universe, who designed me to reflect Your character.

Lord, I consider it a benefit to be in Your lineage. I delight in having You as my heavenly Father. You give me strength to find victory in difficult situations. In easy times or in difficult ones, I know that I benefit from my walk with You. Regardless of the circumstances, may my disposition be one that recognizes the everlasting happiness I have in knowing You.

ON AUTOPILOT

Learn to do well; seek judgment,
relieve the oppressed, judge the fatherless,
plead for the widow.
ISAIAH 1:17

Lord, I was driving when I realized with a start that I'd passed my turn. I'd taken the same route to work so often that on the weekend, when my destination was in the same direction, I'd continued on as if going to work. I was on autopilot, not thinking of my purpose or where I was going.

Father, in my spiritual life, I sometimes go on autopilot. I unconsciously let religious ceremonies and thoughtless worship substitute for honest and meaningful living. Serving You can cause weariness for me and those around me when it becomes a ritual. Help me develop enthusiasm and delight for a conscious Christian walk.

LIVING WORDS

*And thou shalt teach them diligently
unto thy children, and shalt talk of them
when thou sittest in thine house, and when
thou walkest by the way, and when thou
liest down, and when thou risest up.*
DEUTERONOMY 6:7

Father, I know that You call upon me to teach my children Your law. It is easy for me to tell my children what to do if I think I do not have to do it myself.

Father, help me be like Jesus, who illustrated His powerful sermons with examples of love, compassion, and humility. I want my children to receive good training by examples of my actions. May I demonstrate Your love in my daily routine. Lord, write Your commandments on my life so they will be a living lesson to my children.

JOY IN THE JOURNEY

Thou preparest a table before me in the presence of mine enemies: thou anointest my head with oil; my cup runneth over.
PSALM 23:5

Dear Lord, when I was a child, my father drove me along a road toward where a rainbow seemed to end just over the next hill. But no matter how far we traveled, we never reached the end of the rainbow. It was always ahead of us. Later, as an adult, I discovered that no matter what I achieved, contentment stayed out of reach.

Father, thank You for showing me that contentment is not a destination but a journey. Rather than becoming discontent and looking for a better situation, I pray I will focus on what You have given me. May I see my cup as running over with Your blessings.

THE IMPOSSIBLE

And he said, The things which are impossible with men are possible with God.
Luke 18:27

Father, some goals do appear unattainable to me. Yet, I see that even what was impossible a few hundred years ago has become possible today: steamships, airplanes, rockets to the moon, computers, smartphones, and the internet were all once considered wildly fanciful, impractical—or basically impossible.

If these things can be done with the natural abilities You have given us, how much more is possible when You equip us to act in spiritual matters! Father, help me to never hesitate to begin a good work because it appears unlikely to succeed. Help me remember that I am not acting alone. You are at my side. Dear Lord, give me a faith that learns to trust You more each day.

HOPE

And Joshua said unto them, Fear not, nor be dismayed, be strong and of good courage: for thus shall the Lord do to all your enemies against whom ye fight.
JOSHUA 10:25

Father, sometimes I become despondent. My outlook becomes gloomy. It is as if some of the light has gone out in my life. Yet, such a feeling would only be justified if I were without hope, and that is certainly not the case. Your love, the grace of Jesus Christ, and the guidance of the Holy Spirit are with me.

Father, help me face the challenges before me with boldness. Give me strength to shake off anything that troubles my mind so that I can press on each day with a clear purpose. Help me ignore any troubling concerns that might slow my steps.

RIGHTEOUS PERSUASION

When the righteous are in authority,
the people rejoice: but when the wicked
beareth rule, the people mourn.
PROVERBS 29:2

Guide me, Lord, when I am responsible for launching an activity that requires the participation of others. Help me to exercise energy and enthusiasm in enlisting their participation. May I study and test ideas so I will be respected as a source of advice. I do not want a discussion to be a contest I must win but rather a validation that I am applying Christian principles to the issue. Remind me that I can be right and yet be ineffective if I fail to act out of love. Allow my tone, temper, and manner to flow from my devotion to Your truth.

WALKING WITH GOD

Noah was a just man and perfect in his generations, and Noah walked with God.
GENESIS 6:9

Lord, I am defined by whom I choose as my heroes and whom I pattern my life after. Others interpret my character by those with whom I walk. I want to be like the heroes of old, those men of renown in the Old Testament who were described as having "walked with God."

Dear Father, give me the determination to walk at Your side. I seek an honorable walk that shows Your power and character. I know that I am not walking alone; You are with me. I have victory over impossible circumstances because I have placed myself in Your footsteps.

LISTENING

Be still, and know that I am God: I will be exalted among the heathen, I will be exalted in the earth.
PSALM 46:10

Sometimes, Lord, training merely makes me feel bad because after learning what I should do, I realize that I fall far short of perfection. For example, to communicate well, I should listen first. But rather than listening, I am sometimes merely exercising patience while waiting to talk. I should be attentive with my whole mind and body, and I should exchange ideas as well as words.

Father, please help me use my best listening skills when I come before You. Give me the patience to wait for Your message. Help me not be so anxious to put what I consider urgent matters before You first. May I tune in to You with my mind and heart.

A SONG OF PRAISE

The LORD is my strength and my shield;
my heart trusted in him, and I am helped:
therefore my heart greatly rejoiceth;
and with my song will I praise him.
PSALM 28:7

I sing to You, O Lord, a continual song of praise. I declare Your name to all those who come into my presence. Words of thanksgiving are forever upon my lips. I can sing a new song because of Your grace and power.

Your holy name is exalted in heaven and on earth, O Lord Most High. Your righteousness causes my heart to rejoice and break forth in a song of praise: "Glory to the God of my salvation. The generosity of Your compassion overwhelms my soul."

FOR BOLDNESS

And in nothing terrified by your adversaries:
which is to them an evident token of perdition,
but to you of salvation, and that of God.
PHILIPPIANS 1:28

Dear Lord, each day I encounter people who have chosen to walk a path that conflicts with Your laws and those of our government. Their goals are contrary to honest living, and they identify me as their adversary. I pray for fearlessness born of confidence in Your protection as I confront evil.

Father, You give me boldness greater than my natural ability. I walk by Your side, and with Your strength I overcome the fear of what others might do to me. Help me develop strength of spirit, physical courage, and the intelligence to rightly employ them when they are required.

AUTUMN

Be ye ashamed, O ye husbandmen; howl, O ye vinedressers, for the wheat and for the barley; because the harvest of the field is perished.
JOEL 1:11

Father, it's autumn again, and I'm mowing the leaves, trying to mulch them so they go away. I think of autumn as the end season, especially after the first killing frost. Whatever my outdoor goals for the year, they need to be finished by now.

Lord, I wonder what my attitude would be without autumn to remind me of the passage of time. Would I feel any urgency if the air didn't turn crisp and leaves didn't fall from the trees? In Your wisdom, You have created autumn to remind me that I must act now before it is too late. Father, help me develop a sense of urgency for the spiritual harvest.

SYNCHRONIZE

*And God said, Let there be lights in the
firmament of the heaven to divide the day
from the night; and let them be for signs,
and for seasons, and for days, and years.*
GENESIS 1:14

I've stopped wearing a watch, Lord, not because time
is no longer important to me, but because everywhere I go, clocks, watches, and electronic gadgets
constantly show the time. My phone, microwave, car
radio, and computer screen display the time. The
time is everywhere!

Lord, You created time and gave us the dependable progression of the sun, moon, and stars to mark
off days, seasons, and years. Help me recognize each
moment as a gift from You. I pray that I will plan my
day to be in sync with Your eternal purposes.

A TO-DO LIST
CHRISTIAN

To every thing there is a season, and a time
to every purpose under the heaven.
ECCLESIASTES 3:1

I am a to-do list person, Lord. The multitude of those activities threaten to spill into the time I have set aside for prayer. I've moved prayer to category one—an absolutely, positively, must-do activity. Forgive me when taking time to talk to You does not come automatically and naturally.

Father, You'll notice the pad of paper at my side as I come to You in prayer. When unfinished items intrude on my mind, I'll write them down and set them aside so that I can concentrate on talking with You. I am thankful that we have this time to spend together.

UNSAYING WORDS

If any man among you seem to be religious, and bridleth not his tongue, but deceiveth his own heart, this man's religion is vain.
JAMES 1:26

My email software has an option to "unread" an email. Although I don't know any specific purpose for such a feature, I do wish for an "unsay" option for my mouth. I am often dismayed at what I say and regret that the words cannot be taken back.

Lord, I pray that I will put my mind in gear before putting my mouth in motion. Instead of causing division and hurt, let my words uplift and bless. I pray that my conversations will bring unity and hope.

GOD RELIANCE

The LORD is nigh unto them that are of a broken heart; and saveth such as be of a contrite spirit.
PSALM 34:18

Dear Lord, when a friend sees my distress and offers his support, my tendency is to wave him away and assure him that nothing is required from him. I think I can take care of myself.

Father, I am also reluctant to pray about those burdens that I think I should be able to handle without Your help. Help me realize that no matter how independent I may wish to be, I must come to You with a humble and contrite heart. Forgive me for my attempts at self-sufficiency, and show me how to accept help from others and from You.

WEARING A MASK

For the word of God is quick, and powerful,
and sharper than any twoedged sword. . .
and is a discerner of the thoughts
and intents of the heart.
HEBREWS 4:12

Father, as a child I enjoyed putting on a disguise and pretending to be one of my heroes. Playacting did not end with childhood. As an adult, I modify my behavior to match the situation. My choice of language, how I conduct myself, and the clothes I wear conform to what I imagine will help me fit in with my peers. Stress develops when the image I try to project differs from my true self.

Father, I am always visible to You. May I develop the humility to put off the disguise and work instead toward being the person You want me to be.

BY HIS POWER

Humble yourselves in the sight of the Lord,
and he shall lift you up.
JAMES 4:10

As I walk along an ocean's shoreline and see the numerous grains of sand, they remind me, gracious Lord, of Your infinite nature. As I listen to the endless crash of the surf against the shore, the pounding of the waves declares Your power. You have authority over the wind and waves. The unseen forces You created bring in the tides and stir up the restless sea.

Father, I am humbled in the presence of Your creation. I acknowledge You as master of my life. I submit my will to You and dedicate myself to honoring Your name and glorifying Your greatness.

IMPATIENCE

But we glory in tribulations also:
knowing that tribulation worketh patience.
ROMANS 5:3

Dear Father, impatience is one of my faults. I am intolerant of delays at work, irritated when family members do not share my urgency, and restless in the face of inaction. Sometimes I impatiently decide You are not going to solve a problem, and I act outside Your will. I make ill-considered decisions and take reckless actions that endanger me physically and spiritually.

Father, I trust in You. I pray that Your inner peace will sustain me. My goal is neither the impatience of rash actions nor the inaction of passive resignation, but the endurance of a mature Christian who awaits Your will.

SHARPENING THE SAW

I have taught thee in the way of wisdom;
I have led thee in right paths.
PROVERBS 4:11

Lord, even after I sharpened my chain saw, it still wasn't cutting too well. When the chain came off, I realized the problem—I had put the chain on backward.

Father, in my business life, my personal life, and my spiritual life, I understand the importance of investing in myself. I need to learn new skills, try different approaches, and improve myself physically, mentally, and spiritually. But a sharp saw is not enough. Even after I hone my talents, I must use them properly. May I always use them in a way that reaps the most benefit for Your kingdom.

A CLUTTERED MIND

Wherefore seeing we also are compassed about with so great a cloud of witnesses, let us lay aside every weight, and the sin which doth so easily beset us, and let us run with patience the race that is set before us.
HEBREWS 12:1

Father, I'm trying to clean out the garage again. It's amazing the amount of clutter that accumulates in a year's time. Sometimes I become emotionally involved with inanimate objects and delay letting them go. Yet, I discard them when I realize they are taking up space without providing any benefit.

In the same way, I pray I will frequently take a spiritual inventory and make a determined effort to eliminate the mental clutter from my life. Many items need to be set aside: prejudices, dependencies, destructive relationships, jealousies, irrational fears, and memories of past failures. Father, rather than merely moving this clutter to a temporary storage place, help me abandon it entirely.

MATURING

But godliness with contentment is great gain.
1 Timothy 6:6

Father, as a teenager I dreamed of owning a big, four-wheel-drive pickup truck. I imagined how it would impress the girl who took my order in the drive-thru at the fast-food restaurant. Today I smile at my juvenile attempts to get the attention of someone whose name I can no longer remember. Yet, I still fall into the trap of trying to impress people with my possessions.

Lord, I humbly pray that I will be content with the blessings You give me. Focus my thoughts on living a life dedicated to You. Remind me that I am not defined by the things that I own. Almighty God, I am delighted to have You as my provider.

A RESOLUTE HEART

*But Daniel purposed in his heart that he would
not defile himself with the portion of the king's
meat, nor with the wine which he drank: therefore
he requested of the prince of the eunuchs
that he might not defile himself.*
DANIEL 1:8

Heavenly Father, despite the quiet time I am experiencing now, I know that challenges will test me—if not later today then sometime soon. Once temptations are upon me, there is seldom adequate time or the proper environment to make a reasoned response. My goal is to look ahead, consider the evils I may face, and make the right decision before the events occur.

Even so, Lord, after I make an important decision, there is a time of second-guessing, both from myself and from others. Rid my mind of doubts that serve no useful end. I pray I will be resolute and boldly live a consistent, purposeful life.

A GOOD REPUTATION

*Moreover he must have a good report of
them which are without; lest he fall into
reproach and the snare of the devil.*
1 TIMOTHY 3:7

Father, I carry two names—my own and "Christian."
Help me develop a good reputation that brings honor
to You and other Christians. Only You can soften
my character and reset it in the mold You desire.
Although I cannot live a perfect life, Lord, help me to
have a good reputation by following the guidelines
set forth in the Bible.

Lord, I cannot help but be aware that it is difficult to recover a good reputation once it has been
tarnished. Please help me keep Your presence in my
life, and deliver me from the evil forces that would
destroy my name.

CHOICES

That he would grant unto us, that we being delivered out of the hand of our enemies might serve him without fear, in holiness and righteousness before him, all the days of our life.
LUKE 1:74–75

Father, I have seen that accidents occur when a person tries to accomplish two tasks at the same time. Often, neither one is done well, and sometimes the balancing act of trying to achieve two different goals leads to disaster.

In Your Word I read about the impossibility of serving two masters. I commit to You my time, talent, money, and physical and emotional energy. I pray that I will be single-minded so that when a situation calls for action, I will not hesitate to serve You.

A SENSE OF WONDER

Ye are our epistle written in our hearts,
known and read of all men.
2 CORINTHIANS 3:2

Lord, Your Word is a light that guides me to righteousness. It contains wonderful poetry and soul-stirring songs. I read in it exciting stories of heroes of the faith. I marvel at its miraculous events, almost beyond human comprehension. Each day of reading the Bible is a new adventure and a wonderful journey.

I pray, Father, that I will always have a sense of wonder when I read Your Word, that it will always be fresh and illuminate my life. I pray that I will read Your Word, contemplate Your message, and keep it in my mind throughout each day.

ATTACKING PROBLEMS

And the Lord shall deliver me from every evil work, and will preserve me unto his heavenly kingdom.
2 TIMOTHY 4:18

Lord, sometimes I look at problems out of the corner of my eye and pretend they are not there. I choose to ignore them, and they grow more serious because of my inattention. Whether they are big or small, I pray that I will accept challenges with a willing heart that will give me a greater chance of success. Help me attack problems before they attack me.

At times, it appears victory is a tiny island in a vast sea of trials. Sometimes I fail, but help me accept failure as an opportunity to try again with more experience. I pray that I will achieve worthy goals while changing for the better.

BEYOND SELF

*Not that I speak in respect of want:
for I have learned, in whatsoever
state I am, therewith to be content.*
PHILIPPIANS 4:11

Sometimes, Lord, I pray with a selfish agenda. I pray for a new job with better pay. I ask for a new house. I beg for a new truck. When I focus on my wants and not on my needs, I realize my priorities are misplaced. I forget to look upward to seek Your will for my life.

All-knowing God, You see the larger picture, and You have the best interest for my future in view. Teach me, Lord, to keep my eyes on You and then to look outward and extend a hand to those who are truly in need.

STUDY

Study to shew thyself approved unto God,
a workman that needeth not to be ashamed,
rightly dividing the word of truth.
2 TIMOTHY 2:15

Lord, I see examples of Your love in nature. I think about the time I waded across the Mississippi River where it begins as a small stream flowing from Lake Itasca in Minnesota. All along its course, other streams and rivers flow into it so that by the time it reaches the Gulf of Mexico, the stream has become a mighty river.

Lord, just as the tributaries increase the volume of the river, I pray that the living water of Your Word will flow into my life. Although I feel inadequate in Your kingdom, I believe You will allow me to accomplish much for Your glory as I gain knowledge from studying the Bible.

HONOR

And he said unto him, Behold now, there is in this city a man of God, and he is an honourable man; all that he saith cometh surely to pass: now let us go thither; peradventure he can shew us our way that we should go.
1 SAMUEL 9:6

Thank You, Lord, for the place of honor You give me in Your kingdom. As armor helps keep a warrior safe in battle, You shield me from the fiery darts of evil. It is Your assistance that makes it possible for me to live an honorable life. I need Your protective covering to cast off the works of darkness.

Lord, help me live a consistent life so that those who don't know You will be drawn to You. I pray that I will have a good name in the community and that I will direct others to heaven.

PRAISE IN
THE ASSEMBLY

*To appoint unto them that mourn in Zion,
to give unto them beauty for ashes, the oil of joy
for mourning, the garment of praise for the spirit
of heaviness. . .that he might be glorified.*
ISAIAH 61:3

Thank You, Lord, that in Your wisdom You have given me Your day as a reminder to rest and renew. As I assemble with other believers, the stresses of the week dissipate. I feel Your living Spirit as the unified body of Christ worships You.

I thank You, Lord, for allowing me to be a part of the assembly, where the cares of the week are put aside. There is joy in my heart as I leave Your house. Fellowship with other believers ignites a fire that burns in my heart throughout the week.

GOD'S WONDERFUL CREATION

I will praise thee, O Lᴏʀᴅ, with my whole heart;
I will shew forth all thy marvellous works.
I will be glad and rejoice in thee: I will sing
praise to thy name, O thou most High.
Psᴀʟᴍ 9:1–2

Dear Lord, during the early morning of a day I spent in the desert, insects crawled into the blossoms of a hedgehog cactus. At midday, a red-tailed hawk rested on a tall saguaro and watched for an incautious lizard to dart from its shade beneath a rock. Late in the evening I observed a hungry coyote eating fruit that had dropped to the ground from a date palm.

Father God, I watched in fascination as life managed to survive and even thrive despite the harsh environment. I rejoiced in the wonder that I saw in Your created earth. May I too survive and thrive in Your love.

TALENTS

*But now hath God set the members every one
of them in the body, as it hath pleased him.*
1 CORINTHIANS 12:18

Heavenly Father, when I listen to heartfelt singing at church, glory from heaven seems to be radiating from each singer's lips. Even my off-key notes do not distract from our praises.

When it comes to singing, I admire the talents of others and realize how limited I am. But, Lord, in Your Word I read how You give each person a different capacity. You have designed me to be a unique individual. My talents may seem less significant than those of others, but I want to use the abilities that I do have for Your glory.

FOOD FOR THOUGHT

As newborn babes, desire the sincere milk
of the word, that ye may grow thereby.
1 PETER 2:2

Dear Lord, as a new Christian, I read the Bible to gain spiritual maturity. Unlike my physical body, my spiritual maturity can continue to grow throughout my life. Yes, reading the Bible provides spiritual food for my soul. It helps me grow. But just as importantly, it repairs the damage done by living in a world where each day brings challenges to my Christian character.

O God, now that I am further along in my walk with You, I recognize that the world produces wear and tear on my spiritual body. It must be repaired and given fresh energy by daily renewal through Your Word.

DRIFTING ALONG

And said unto them, Why sleep ye?
rise and pray, lest ye enter into temptation.
LUKE 22:46

Lord, I always enjoy going on a canoe trip. As I drift along with my face turned toward the sun and my fingers running through the cool water, I sometimes grow sleepy. Then, suddenly, I become fully awake as my canoe is caught in the roar of rapids.

Lord Jesus, sometimes I find myself drifting in my spiritual journey. My interest in relationships with other Christians weakens, and my interest in sharing the Gospel diminishes. I feel a false sense of security, and I stop paddling toward the safer channel. Awake me, Lord Jesus, and keep me from drifting into the dangers of this world.

WORRY

Which of you by taking thought can add one cubit unto his stature?
MATTHEW 6:27

Father, thanks for calming my agitation in times of distress. With Your peace, I smile at my foolish concerns: Some situations are already passed and cannot be changed; others were unlikely to happen; some were trivial and not worth my emotional energy—but worry turned a small concern into a long shadow. I could have changed only a few of the situations that troubled me.

Divine Father, equip me to deal with the problems over which I can make a difference. I pray that I will see my troubles more clearly with Your wisdom.

A FIRM FOUNDATION

The LORD is my rock, and my fortress, and my deliverer; my God, my strength, in whom I will trust; my buckler, and the horn of my salvation, and my high tower.
PSALM 18:2

Lord, the trilobite fossil I keep on my desk reminds me of the enduring quality of rocks. This imprint of an extinct marine animal has lasted thousands of years since its body was cast as stone.

Everlasting Lord, You are the spiritual rock that endures throughout all ages. You keep me from sinking in the quagmire of my sins. I want to be dedicated to following Your Word and building my life on the firm foundation of Jesus. I ask that You mold me into an earthly resemblance of Your likeness.

MAKING MISTAKES

As far as the east is from the west, so far hath he removed our transgressions from us.
PSALM 103:12

Father, I am always making mistakes. As a child, I used an eraser to rub out the errors and correct them, although the erasures were obvious on the paper. More recently, I used touch-up paint to cover scratches on doorframes, although getting the paints to match exactly was impossible.

O Lord, I sometimes make bad judgments and sin against You. Within my own power, I cannot correct those mistakes, but I trust in Jesus to blot out all my iniquities. When You remove them, You don't leave a smudgy erasure or a mismatched touch-up. Thank You for removing them entirely so they no longer exist.

TAKE REFUGE

Trust in him at all times; ye people, pour out your heart before him: God is a refuge for us.
PSALM 62:8

Heavenly Father, I know that storms are a part of life. I remember hiking in the Rocky Mountains when a cold rain started. We were prepared for the rain but not for the hail that followed. Since we were above the tree line, we had to scramble across a boulder field to find shelter beneath an overhanging rock. We were happy to find a safe place until the storm passed.

Father, I often think I am prepared for the storms of life that lash out at me, but then they become more severe than I anticipated. Thank You, Lord, for providing a safe haven for me. Lord Jesus, I am glad to have You as my spiritual shelter. My soul will never be in jeopardy as long as I take refuge in You.

LONG-HAUL ENDURANCE

For the which cause I also suffer these things:
nevertheless I am not ashamed: for I know whom
I have believed, and am persuaded that he is
able to keep that which I have committed
unto him against that day.
2 Timothy 1:12

Lord, when my duties and obligations become too much for me, I ask why I must endure them. Yet, I read Your Word and understand that when I am beaten down, I am not defeated. Minor problems are opportunities for growth and prepare me for the major crises I will surely face along the way. You are equipping me to succeed despite momentary setbacks.

Prepare me to endure, not for a moment but for a lifetime. Teach me to develop the stamina to overcome not only momentary challenges but also trials that may last a lifetime.

A SPIRIT OF COURAGE

For God hath not given us the spirit of fear;
but of power, and of love, and of a sound mind.
2 TIMOTHY 1:7

Father, fear and anxiety are twin thieves that rob me of my tranquility. I can't sleep, I can't eat, and I can't think. Fear saps my strength, muddles my mind, and weakens my spirit. Fear is always there, lurking in the shadows, ready to snatch away my willingness to confront challenges.

Lord, I pray that courage would dominate my fears so that I may be undaunted and uncowed. Prayer and study of Your Word will build my courage because knowledge and love overcome fear. Grant me confidence and a clear head when it is time for me to choose between courage and fear, truth and lies, right and wrong.

DYNAMIC LEADERSHIP

*Stand therefore, having your loins girt about
with truth, and having on the breastplate
of righteousness; and your feet shod with
the preparation of the gospel of peace.*
Ephesians 6:14–15

Father, when I am called upon to be a leader, I sometimes feel that I am not the one best equipped to lead. Grant me the capacity to confront this apprehension and overcome it. When making decisions, may I always listen to others so they will gladly participate in our common goal. Equip me to follow Your guidance and direction so that I select the right course of action.

I know that my leadership may not be universally accepted. Let me be unflinching in carrying out my work, despite criticism. May I lead by example and with a humble attitude.

DELIGHT

*And not only so, but we also joy in God through
our Lord Jesus Christ, by whom we have
now received the atonement.*
ROMANS 5:11

All joy comes from You, Lord. I can experience joy
because of the risen Christ. I no longer have the
heavy weight of my transgressions to discourage
me. Your joy lifts my spirit and relieves my anxieties.
Thank You, Lord, for joy that gives me strength to
run this spiritual race.

Lord, for my joy to be fully realized, I must share
it with others. My desire is to let joy, a fruit of the
Spirit, flourish in my life. Help me bless others by
allowing You to shine on them through my life.

FOR GOVERNMENT LEADERS

*I exhort therefore, that, first of all, supplications,
prayers, intercessions, and giving of thanks,
be made for all men; for kings, and for all that
are in authority; that we may lead a quiet and
peaceable life in all godliness and honesty.*
1 TIMOTHY 2:1–2

Heavenly Father, I ask that You guide the leaders
of my country. May they have integrity, morality,
and leadership ability. Guide them to extend Your
influence into all areas of society. Empower them
to overcome the dark forces at work in the world.

Father, I ask for Your guidance upon my government's leaders. Direct them to take our nation in the
way You would have us go. Help them realize that
true prosperity comes only through the application
of Christian values. May the laws they make uphold
and protect our right to worship You.

SYNERGY

Be of the same mind one toward another. Mind not high things, but condescend to men of low estate. Be not wise in your own conceits.
ROMANS 12:16

Lord, wonderful moments occur when I work so well with another person that we seem to act as one individual. Our ideas function perfectly together, and our progress toward our goal goes more quickly than our individual efforts would. We have a shared objective, and we use our different talents to accomplish our unified purpose.

Father, please help me recognize that differences between people are not negative but positive. Give me the insight to see how I can harmonize with them to make a pleasing whole. Guide me to be a cooperative individual as I work within Your kingdom.

EMERGENCY WORKERS

Defend the poor and fatherless:
do justice to the afflicted and needy.
PSALM 82:3

Almighty God, I pray for those who respond to emergencies, whether police, firefighters, or medical personnel. Please protect these public servants as they come to the rescue of those in dangerous situations. Provide them with the courage and wisdom to extricate others and themselves from the scenes of crisis.

Guide our police as they make split-second decisions in emotionally charged situations. Watch over our firefighters as their jobs take them into harm's way. Give our medical personnel skillful hands and clear minds as they rush to save lives. Grant all of these individuals the ability to act quickly and compassionately.

YOUTH AND VIGOR

*Lo, I am this day fourscore and five years old.
As yet I am as strong this day as I was in the day
that Moses sent me: as my strength was
then, even so is my strength now.*
JOSHUA 14:10–11

Heavenly Father, when I stepped out on my own as a young man, I was naive and inexperienced, uncertain of my own future, and erratic in my course. When I looked to older men as role models, I saw individuals who had become cynical and world-weary, no longer believing that they could make a difference. Somewhere between those two extremes lies the confident and vigorous man I want to be.

Dear Lord, give me an enthusiastic and vigorous mind, regardless of my age. Help me to renew and refresh myself by reading about the men of the Bible, those men of renown, who continued to follow You with youthful vigor despite their advancing years.

LAUGHTER

A merry heart doeth good like a medicine:
but a broken spirit drieth the bones.
PROVERBS 17:22

Heavenly Father, I know that You want me to be joyful. A glad heart cannot help but reveal itself with a ready smile. How can I feel joy without smiling, and how can I smile without breaking out in laughter? Although there are times to be somber, I realize that reacting to every event with the utmost seriousness can produce a joyless life. May I never present myself with exaggerated dignity.

Father, as a joy-filled person, may I offer an easy smile and an honest laugh that encourage people to spend time in my presence. I pray I will always have a joyful outlook that lightens my life and the lives of those around me.

COUNTING BLESSINGS

Enter into his gates with thanksgiving,
and into his courts with praise: be thankful
unto him, and bless his name.
PSALM 100:4

Dear Lord, what bountiful harvest I have received from You! I count blessings without number. You have given me health, a warm family life, prosperity, and a peaceful heart. You have given me strength in adversity and security in turmoil. You have given me opportunities to serve and thereby enriched my life.

I acknowledge the rich blessings that You have showered upon me. Help me appreciate them. Remove from my heart the idea that my recognition of these blessings will earn me future blessings. Let me focus on what You have done for me and rejoice in all the daily blessings You give me.

ATTITUDE

Create in me a clean heart, O God;
and renew a right spirit within me.
PSALM 51:10

Father, I am quick to focus on those things that affect me most directly. Often, I confess, I improperly view my wants as essentials. From minor matters such as restaurant service to more important ones such as making major purchases, I insist that my so-called requirements be fully met. I think and act as if those serving me should put my needs first.

Lord, keep a check on my attitude. I want to have a friendly disposition when I deal with others. Create in me a calm, controlled temperament. Help me have a "can do," "everything's okay" attitude rather than a "me" attitude.

ENCOURAGING THOSE WHO SERVE

But charge Joshua, and encourage him, and strengthen him: for he shall go over before this people, and he shall cause them to inherit the land which thou shalt see.
DEUTERONOMY 3:28

Lord, just as You instructed Moses to encourage Joshua to lead Your people across the Jordan River to enter the Promised Land, help me encourage those who have been chosen to serve. Help me ease their burdens and give them the will to continue the work You have called them to do.

When I am leading others, may I always be mindful of my role as Your servant. Help me choose the right words and actions to revitalize others when they have grown weary, assure them when they have doubts, console them in times of apparent failure, and reward them with heartfelt praise for their successes.

GET OVER IT

And when ye stand praying, forgive, if ye have ought against any: that your Father also which is in heaven may forgive you your trespasses.
MARK 11:25

Sometimes, Lord, my mind wanders back to earlier in my life. For some reason, injustices immediately come to mind more readily than pleasant experiences. Anger surfaces when I dwell on the unfair treatment I experienced. I had many privileged opportunities and blessings, but I remember the negative events with far more emotion than the positive occasions.

Forgiving Lord, help me press on with my life. Reviewing reruns of my past serves no purpose. I will not use past events as an excuse for my current shortcomings. With Your help, I will release the resentments I am carrying and accept responsibility for my own actions.

GROWING IN FORGIVENESS

For thus saith the LORD of hosts; After the glory hath he sent me unto the nations which spoiled you: for he that toucheth you toucheth the apple of his eye.
ZECHARIAH 2:8

Heavenly Father, I am struck by references in the Old Testament that describe Your people as the apple of Your eye. I realize that I am very precious in Your sight. If I am the apple of Your eye, then I must replicate Your characteristics to be a true offspring of Yours, just as apples reproduce seeds like those from which they originated.

Lord, since I am Your offspring, I need to compare my righteousness to You and not to others. Help me to grow in Your likeness by freely forgiving the offenses of others.

NO FREE LUNCH

For by grace are ye saved through faith;
and that not of yourselves: it is the gift of God:
not of works, lest any man should boast.
EPHESIANS 2:8–9

Lord, because I have heard the statement "There is no such thing as a free lunch" so often, I view with skepticism anything that is offered for free. Even accepting Your grace is difficult. But You have overcome my reluctance by showing that although grace is free to me, it did come at a price. If I do not accept Your grace, then Jesus' death for me was in vain.

Father, I have become a privileged child, receiving favors and divine protection merely by accepting Your gift of salvation. You have delivered me from the captivity of sin and restored me to a life of freedom. Thank You, Lord.

THE GROWTH OF SIN

Then when lust hath conceived,
it bringeth forth sin: and sin, when it
is finished, bringeth forth death.
JAMES 1:15

Dear Lord, during a visit to the Everglades, I saw a hammock tree that was being slowly strangled by a fig tree. Months earlier, a bird dropped a tiny fig seed that lodged in the hammock's branches. The fig tree sprouted and began sending its roots earthward, spiraling around the hammock tree. Eventually the death-hug of the fig tree will prevail and destroy its host.

Father, I often ignore sinful practices until they become dangerous to my spiritual life. For sin to flourish, it must be nourished by the very person it is harming. May I ever be alert to sin's influence and rely on Your help to conquer it.

ROOTED IN JESUS

As ye have therefore received Christ Jesus the Lord, so walk ye in him: rooted and built up in him, and stablished in the faith, as ye have been taught, abounding therein with thanksgiving.
COLOSSIANS 2:6–7

As I hiked along a wilderness trail today, Lord, I stepped over some tree roots projecting above the ground. I was reminded of the importance of good root systems. I could not see most of the roots, but I could see the tall trees they supported. Without a strong root system, the trees could not stand upright. The trunk and branches above the ground could not survive without the water and nutrients provided by the roots.

Lord, Your creation provides me with visual applications to my spiritual life. I need to be rooted in Your Word to be a strong, stable Christian. You, Lord Jesus, are the water and food that I seek to support my spiritual life and health.

SECURITY IN THE LORD

*And they that know thy name will put their
trust in thee: for thou, L<small>ORD</small>, hast not
forsaken them that seek thee.*
P<small>SALM</small> 9:10

Each morning, Lord, I read the business section of
the newspaper. The economic future looks bright
one day, but the next day projections are bleak.
I carefully invest my meager resources, but the
fluctuating interest rates and an unstable stock
market make me wary. None of the choices I make
are completely free of risk. Things can go drastically
wrong in a heartbeat.

Lord, I am unable to see what the future holds,
but I do trust You as the One who holds the future.
Life's wealth comes and goes. My security is in You,
my provider.

BEYOND THE MUNDANE

Therefore, my beloved brethren, be ye stedfast, unmoveable, always abounding in the work of the Lord, forasmuch as ye know that your labour is not in vain in the Lord.
1 CORINTHIANS 15:58

Dear Father, contentment and satisfaction are a small step apart. I pray that I will never be too satisfied with myself or become too comfortable in my situation. May my contentment be one of action instead of ease.

Lord, I ask You to show me the doors of opportunity that I can open to grow and improve. Should I refuse to open those doors, then jar me out of my routine and force me out of my comfort zone. If I do exactly the same thing each day in exactly the same way, then I should not expect results any different from the day before. Help me push beyond the mundane into the realm of active service.

SELF-HELP

*The word of the Lord endureth for ever.
And this is the word which by the
gospel is preached unto you.*
1 PETER 1:25

Father, around the office I see people carrying self-help books to read during their lunch breaks. Each month another title makes the bestseller list. Yet, few have enough substance to be enduring classics.

Lord, when I study my human nature, I find many constants in my character—I am sinful, selfish, full of pride, sometimes afraid, and always facing death. The Bible addresses all these issues. Your Word is more thorough than any contemporary book that would try to show me how to improve myself without Your assistance. May I always remember to turn to Your enduring guidebook for daily living and eternal salvation.

TEMPERANCE

But the fruit of the Spirit is love, joy, peace, longsuffering, gentleness, goodness, faith, meekness, temperance: against such there is no law.
GALATIANS 5:22–23

Father, when I sit down to eat, I find it difficult to have self-restraint. Not only do I have problems controlling my appetite for food, but I also have weaknesses in many other areas of my life. Exercising temperance is a challenge. Yet, I know it is a fruit of the Spirit and that I should manifest it in my life.

Lord, I ask You to give me power to govern my thoughts and my actions. I pray for moderation and self-restraint in my personal conduct.

GRACE

*Wherefore we receiving a kingdom
which cannot be moved, let us have grace,
whereby we may serve God acceptably
with reverence and godly fear.*
HEBREWS 12:28

Father, I know that I cannot obtain absolute perfection in my life. I appeal to You for Your mercy. I know that Your forgiveness is without limit, provided I exercise the same forgiveness with others. I pray for the help of the Holy Spirit so I can forgive repeatedly without harboring resentment.

Thank You for Your generous grace. I ask that Your mercy flow over me. I pray that You will favor my undertakings and wrap them in Your clemency so that even when I fail, I will be under Your protection.

FOR MERCY

Be merciful unto me, O Lord:
for I cry unto thee daily.
PSALM 86:3

Father, sometimes You seem to be far from me. I look and see a great abyss between us, but as I pray, my vision clears and I perceive a bridge that was there all along. It is a bridge of mercy constructed by You. Thank You for building the bridge that connects me to the peace You provide.

Sometimes I think I am not worthy of mercy and question how You can offer it to me. Implant in me the understanding that to appreciate Your mercy, I must show mercy to others. Banish from my heart the evil thought that others are not worthy of Your forgiving compassion.

OF PRAISE

His glory covered the heavens,
and the earth was full of his praise.
HABAKKUK 3:3

Almighty Father of all creation, accept this prayer of praise. I respect You, venerate You, and honor You as the Creator of the universe and everything in it. I recognize You as my maker. I am thankful that You were too kind to create the world and then walk away from it. Instead, You take an interest in my daily life and care about my eternal well-being.

I sometimes hesitate to offer praise because doing so implies that I understand enough of Your power to appreciate it. Despite this misgiving, may I always praise You for Your love, the grace of Jesus, and the guidance of the Holy Spirit.

CROWN OF LIFE

I have fought a good fight, I have finished my course, I have kept the faith: henceforth there is laid up for me a crown of righteousness.
2 TIMOTHY 4:7–8

Father, as I watch television broadcasts of British royalty wearing their jeweled crowns, I cannot help but be impressed with the pomp and ceremony surrounding their public appearances. However, I know that they have lives as brief as mine. They will die, leaving behind their riches.

Father, help me focus on the One who wore the crown of thorns. That terrible crown is gone now, but Jesus is still alive. I look forward to wearing the crown of eternal life. Dear Lord, I can never earn that priceless gift. You freely give it to me and all who have been faithful.

INDUSTRIAL-STRENGTH BLEACH

Come now, and let us reason together, saith the Lord: though your sins be as scarlet, they shall be as white as snow; though they be red like crimson, they shall be as wool.
Isaiah 1:18

Father, sometimes I place a pen in my shirt pocket without retracting the point. The mistake causes a prominent ink stain on my shirt. The garment is ruined, only to be worn when I am doing grubby chores.

Unlike the shirt, dear Lord, You are able and willing to cleanse my life that has been tarnished by worldly ambitions. Please remove every sin from my life so that my soul will be white as snow. Remove all bitterness and every desire to do evil. Thank You for creating in me a pure heart, O Lord.

RECHARGE

*Be of good courage, and he shall strengthen
your heart, all ye that hope in the LORD.*
PSALM 31:24

Lord, when my car doesn't start because the battery
is dead, I get a jump start and recharge it. But why
did it run down? Did I leave the lights on, was there a
hidden drain on the battery, or did the battery itself
have a bad cell?

Father, sometimes I am drained of strength.
Thank You for providing opportunities for me to be
recharged by plugging into prayer, Bible study, and
fellowship with other Christians. Help me discover
the reason that I have become spiritually exhausted.
Renew me and help me keep Your abundant power.

WINTER

Thou hast set all the borders of the earth:
thou hast made summer and winter.
PSALM 74:17

When I think of the hallmarks of the winter holiday season—candles, candy, carols, bows, and gifts—the weather doesn't seem as cold. The bother of shoveling snow disappears when I watch children make snow angels. The coldest season is in some ways the warmest one. It is difficult for me to give someone the cold shoulder when I hear the sounds of "Joy to the World."

Father, during the winter months, let me be friendly and bring warmth to others despite the freezing weather outside. May I greet strangers with a smile so sunny that it makes them feel less need for a heavy coat.

TRUST IN GOD

God is our refuge and strength, a very present help in trouble. Therefore will not we fear, though the earth be removed, and though the mountains be carried into the midst of the sea.
Psalm 46:1–2

Father, I prayed for You to quell the doubts and fears that troubled my mind. You gave me guidance to overcome those events that were in my power to change. You gave me the emotional soundness to bear the trials that remained. I see now that You put them there so that, by enduring them, I would gain character and confidence.

Lord, help me recognize the distress of others when they are in a valley. Help me understand their pain and support them through their dark days. Give me the wisdom to be an encouragement to them. May I learn to put my trust in You and succeed in sharing that trust with others.

WIN-WIN

As every man hath received the gift, even so minister the same one to another, as good stewards of the manifold grace of God.
1 PETER 4:10

Lord Most High, sometimes I allow my future to be determined by others. I become dependent upon them to guide me and to take the lead in solving my problems. At other times I try to be totally independent of others and chart my own course. I fail to recognize that You have made human beings to be interdependent. I understand this concept as it applies to the church, my marriage, and family.

Lord, may I recognize the advantages of shared action in my daily contact with other people. I pray that I will not think others must lose in order for me to win. Instead, guide me to succeed in cooperative endeavors that bring glory to Your kingdom.

DESTRUCTIVE DEPENDENCIES

A good man sheweth favour, and lendeth:
he will guide his affairs with discretion.
PSALM 112:5

Heavenly Father, I see destructive dependencies creeping up on me. An innocuous hobby may become an all-consuming interest. Other dependencies are clearly harmful: those of a sexual nature or addictions to narcotics, alcohol, or gambling. They follow a distressing progression: At first I am repelled by them; slowly I begin to tolerate them; then I secretly participate in them; finally I actively promote them.

I become a shell of a person, a ghost ship without a helmsman. The dependencies cause damage not only to me but also to those I love.

Lord, I understand that habits can be good or bad. With Your help I desire to make everything I do a carefully chosen practice rather than an unthinking habit.

WORSHIP

*Nevertheless he left not himself without witness,
in that he did good, and gave us rain from
heaven, and fruitful seasons, filling our
hearts with food and gladness.*
Acts 14:17

Heavenly Father, I looked out this morning to see a steady, soaking rain. I thought of my parched yard and how much the grass needed the precipitation. Within a few minutes, the blades of grass appeared green and glistened with healthy life.

Lord, sometimes I become spiritually dry. Like a drought, the condition creeps in slowly over time. Before my strength grows weak, please send heavenly water to refresh my soul and rejuvenate my worship. I pray that I will always be receptive to You and that Your abundant blessings will continue to shower down on me.

SPREADING THE GOOD NEWS

How beautiful upon the mountains are the feet of
him that bringeth good tidings, that publisheth
peace; that bringeth good tidings of good,
that publisheth salvation; that saith
unto Zion, Thy God reigneth!
ISAIAH 52:7

Father, when I trace on a map the journeys of Jesus and the apostles, I realize that they must have been rugged individuals to withstand the rigors of their travels. Considering that their mode of transportation was usually walking, they must have been physically strong.

My feet are not dusty and callused like theirs, and I don't have the endurance for a long-distance trek, but I do pray for the spiritual strength to live an overcoming life. On my journey with You, Lord, commission me with joy and perseverance to go forth and proclaim the Good News of salvation.

STAYING CONNECTED

And he is the head of the body, the church: who is the beginning, the firstborn from the dead; that in all things he might have the preeminence.
Colossians 1:18

I feel more connected to You, Jesus, when I fellowship with other believers. The house of God provides a plot of fertile soil where my knowledge of You can grow and my soul can be refreshed. Each time I attend church, I acknowledge You as my Savior. It is one way I demonstrate to others my commitment to You.

Lord, I pray I will always look to You as the head of the church.

HEAVENLY COMPASS

*And the very God of peace sanctify you wholly;
and I pray God your whole spirit and soul and
body be preserved blameless unto the
coming of our Lord Jesus Christ.*
1 Thessalonians 5:23

Dear Lord, when I am hiking with my children, I am constantly checking my direction with a compass and a trail guide. The little ones depend on me to set the right course for them. As a compass is drawn to the north, so I am drawn to You, knowing that others follow in my steps.

Heavenly Father, my soul seeks to align with Your mercy and grace. You, O Lord, are my righteous Creator. I pray that I will live a consecrated life through Your enabling power. Please guide me to live right and dispel the negative powers that could draw me off course.

FULLY ARMORED

*Put on the whole armour of God, that ye may be
able to stand against the wiles of the devil.*
EPHESIANS 6:11

Father, when I first gave my life to You, I hungered for
Your Word. Every day I read the Bible and studied it
carefully. Now my mind strays as I read, and I have
to double back and reread passages to comprehend
them. I question how much my mind retains and
wonder what benefits I am receiving. Yet, each day
I eat meals so my body has food to repair tissues
and provide energy for physical activities.

In the same way, I understand that reading Your
Word provides food for my soul. Lord, I pray that I
will always be so hungry for Your Word that I will set
aside time for daily Bible reading.

HUSBAND

Nevertheless let every one of you in particular so love his wife even as himself; and the wife see that she reverence her husband.
EPHESIANS 5:33

Lord, I've heard that a husband prays for You to keep his wife the sweet person he married, and a wife prays for You to change her husband into the man she wants him to be. Instead, I pray that You will make us what You want us to be.

I am thankful, Lord, that I married the woman I loved, and today I can say I love the woman I married. I pray that I will respect her as a faithful partner and that we may walk side by side in the path You direct.

CASTING MY VOTE

If my people, which are called by my name,
shall humble themselves, and pray, and seek my
face, and turn from their wicked ways; then will
I hear from heaven, and will forgive
their sin, and will heal their land.
2 CHRONICLES 7:14

Dear Lord, at each election I cast my ballot and wear the sticker that says "I voted." When I think about my Christian service, I realize that my most influential vote is the way that I live. Each day I make choices: the products I buy, the television programs I surf through, and the church activities I participate in. I vote by my attitudes and actions.

I pray I will vote for justice, honesty, and moral responsibility, not only in the ballot box but also in the daily choices that I make.

RESPECT

*He that followeth after righteousness and mercy
findeth life, righteousness, and honour.*
PROVERBS 21:21

Lord, although I do not often acknowledge it, I realize that my wife's respect is important to me. I see other men who are devastated when they lose the respect of someone they cherish. I have heard that, for some men, being respected is more important than being loved. "Not me, Lord," I say. But I know I can be shattered by a word rashly spoken, especially by my wife.

I pray that I will inspire respect by making sacrifices. Remove from me the idea that my sense of purpose depends on how others view me. Replace it with a concern for how You regard me.

DELIVERANCE FROM CAPTURE

And this I pray. . .That ye may approve things that are excellent; that ye may be sincere and without offence till the day of Christ. Being filled with the fruits of righteousness, which are by Jesus Christ, unto the glory and praise of God.
PHILIPPIANS 1:9–11

Heavenly Father, spiders spin webs to snare wandering insects. Some of the spiderwebs are in such obscure locations, I wonder how an insect will ever be trapped. But the spider knows how to capture unsuspecting victims.

Father, I know that Satan too catches valuable souls in a web of sin. Often the temptation is placed in an unsuspecting location. Lord, guard my mind, spirit, and body from Satan's lures. Deliver me from the temptations to violate Your laws. Only with Your help can I maintain a holy lifestyle and avoid becoming a victim seized by deception.

SPIRITUAL VITAMINS

*My people are destroyed
for lack of knowledge.*
HOSEA 4:6

Heavenly Father, my doctor told me a dietary deficiency was causing the skin to flake off my fingers. Despite robust meals, some essential component was missing from my diet. The doctor recommended that I consume more fish each week to provide the missing ingredient, and the problem disappeared.

Father, if I search through Your Word and read only those passages that I find most agreeable to my preconceived ideas of Your message, then I am missing some of the essential elements that I need for a strong relationship with You. I pray that I will choose to become healthy by accepting all the spiritual vitamins that You have provided me in Your Word.

FIRST THINGS FIRST

*But seek ye first the kingdom of God,
and his righteousness; and all these
things shall be added unto you.*
MATTHEW 6:33

Lord, each day I rush around to finish a multitude of minor tasks that absolutely, positively have to be done by the evening deadline. I am assailed from all sides as if swimming with a school of piranhas. Each one nibbles away at my time. Each task by itself would be a minor distraction, but together, they crowd out important duties.

From Your wisdom, Lord, I want to understand what matters most. Bring order to the chaos of my daily life. Help me identify the proper priorities and organize my life around them.

SETTING GOALS

He hath shewed thee, O man, what is good;
and what doth the Lord require of thee,
but to do justly, and to love mercy,
and to walk humbly with thy God?
Micah 6:8

Father, last year a friend and I set out to hike a mountain trail. We had no particular destination in mind. The grueling trail ended in a field of boulders and an impassable bank of snow. Later we learned of a different route that would have taken us to a spectacular vista at the summit.

Father, I often expend my strength to reach an unworthy goal. No matter how effective I am, if I do not first select a worthy goal, the end result will be disappointing. In my walk with You, I pray that I select the right goal and always keep it firmly before my eyes.

BEING WITH BELIEVERS

*I was glad when they said unto me,
Let us go into the house of the L*ORD.
PSALM 122:1

Heavenly Father, reading the Bible, talking to You in prayer, singing hymns, and meeting with other Christians help fortify my spiritual life. Only by becoming strong in You can I overcome obstacles. I need to assemble with other Christians because I gain strength by associating with those who love You. Our singing, praying, and study of Your Word inspire me to a closer walk with You.

Heavenly Father, I need the fellowship of dedicated believers. Help me realize that they need me too because we are blessed through fellowship with others.

A READY HARVEST

Pray ye therefore the Lord of the harvest, that he will send forth labourers into his harvest.
MATTHEW 9:38

Father, even from my limited gardening experience, I've seen that weeds grow without encouragement, but good crops require attention. Seeds must be planted in soil that has been prepared to receive them, weeds must be eliminated, and produce must be harvested at the right time.

Almighty Savior, I see that the same sequence is necessary to produce a spiritual harvest. Lord, make me a faithful worker in Your harvest. Help me to be diligent in the work that brings the lost to You. May I have an urgency to gather souls into Your kingdom before the season is past and the crop is lost.

ASKING FOR DIRECTIONS

*For even hereunto were ye called: because
Christ also suffered for us, leaving us an
example, that ye should follow his steps.*
1 PETER 2:21

Lord, I would rather drive in circles for an hour than stop for five minutes to ask for directions. Usually I end up with only some lost time, but on some occasions I've ended up in areas that I would normally avoid.

Sometimes I wander around spiritually too. Because I refuse to ask for directions, I find myself in places that I should avoid. Father, I pray that I may be willing to ask for Your guidance and follow it. Protect me from self-reliance and arrogance. Direct me to Your truth and help me act according to Your guidance.

THE POWER
OF THE WORD

*For our gospel came not unto you in word only,
but also in power, and in the Holy Ghost, and in
much assurance; as ye know what manner of
men we were among you for your sake.*
1 THESSALONIANS 1:5

Lord, I confess to You that I often read the Bible hurriedly and without much comprehension. Despite my sometimes superficial reading, I do gain something from staying in touch with You. More gratifying, though, are those occasions when I take the time to think upon Your Word and meditate upon Your message. Most useful of all are those occasions when certain passages capture my attention. For several days I carry the verses around in my thoughts and pray about them. Slowly, by continually holding them in my mind, they dawn into full light.

Father, I pray that the power of Your Word will transform my mind. Change the printed words into words written on my heart and living in my spirit.

LITTLE THINGS

*Behold also the ships, which though they be
so great, and are driven of fierce winds, yet are
they turned about with a very small helm,
whithersoever the governor listeth.*
JAMES 3:4

Father, when I first came to You, I was so determined to do great works that I considered little jobs beneath my effort. When I fell short of my goals, I despaired of ever doing anything for You. All along, a multitude of small deeds have been available, but I ignored them.

Lord, grant me eyes to see tasks that need to be done and a willing heart to do them. In Your name, I ask Your help in using my daily activities to show kindness and concern for others.

PARDON

And I will cleanse them from all their iniquity,
whereby they have sinned against me; and I will
pardon all their iniquities, whereby they
have sinned, and whereby they have
transgressed against me.
JEREMIAH 33:8

Father, there was a time when I had the nagging uncertainty about whether I had been truly forgiven. I had remorse for my sins, I repented of my actions, and I desired to understand the truth of the Gospel. But as a new Christian, I tried unsuccessfully to live up to the contradictory advice I was given.

Today I know that I cannot earn a place in Your kingdom by what I do or avoid doing. Instead, I bring You a heart of obedience and an affection for spiritual matters. I am secure in the knowledge of Your saving grace. I honor You with a heart of obedience and know that when I fail, You will pardon me.

WORTHY OF HONOR

*O Lord our Lord, how excellent is
thy name in all the earth!*
PSALM 8:9

O Lord, I have peered into a microscope and have seen a world in one drop of water. I have gazed through a telescope and have seen stars and galaxies uncountable. When I see the majesty of Your vast creation, I am brought to my knees in wonder. But in my humble admiration, there is also a desperate question: Do You notice me and concern Yourself with me?

I thank You, Lord, for personally answering my question. When I am apprehensive, I put my trust in You, and You keep me safe. When I am lonely, You talk to me. When I am sad, You make me happy. When I am weak, I bow before You and feel Your strength.

COMPLEX TO SIMPLE

I will greatly rejoice in the LORD, my soul shall be joyful in my God; for he hath clothed me with the garments of salvation, he hath covered me with the robe of righteousness, as a bridegroom decketh himself with ornaments.
ISAIAH 61:10

Father, I see the wonder of Your creation in all of its complexity, and I bow before You in humble adoration. When I study the world You have created, I cannot but admire how the complex parts work together as a simple whole.

When I read the Bible and study Your Word, it is at first a complex story that spans the ages. But then I see Your guiding hand behind the events that brought Jesus into this world, and I see how His death and resurrection give salvation to those who simply accept You by faith. I admire and honor You for giving me a simple salvation plan, one that I can comprehend.

A SPECIAL PLANET

He loveth righteousness and judgment:
the earth is full of the goodness of the LORD.
PSALM 33:5

Heavenly Father, the photographs of earth taken from space always cause me to pause because of the stunning beauty they reveal: green forests, brown deserts, white clouds, and blue-green oceans. The earth looks like a marvelous jewel set against the black background of space. It causes me to adore You, Lord, and remember You as the Creator.

Father, I appreciate the earth as Your special creation. Keep me alert to the goodness around me. But help me always be mindful that this earth is not my permanent home. Despite its beauty, the earth is but a way station to a much grander place with You. May I always live my life with the knowledge that heaven is my eventual destination.

THE GOLDEN RULE

Therefore all things whatsoever ye would that men should do to you, do ye even so to them: for this is the law and the prophets.
MATTHEW 7:12

Lord, I have memorized the Bible verse that is called the Golden Rule. Yet putting it into practice is far more difficult than learning the words. While You were here on earth, You demonstrated the perfect example of living out this principle.

Jesus, I praise You for showing me compassion and granting me forgiveness for my transgressions. Thank You for teaching me how to have peace in my life. Lord, give me the determination to do unto others as I want them to do unto me.

NOTHING NEW

*I have seen all the works that are done
under the sun; and, behold, all is
vanity and vexation of spirit.*
Ecclesiastes 1:14

Each day, Lord, I am bombarded with advertisements. Embedded in the glittering generalities is the assurance that the merchandise is on the leading edge. The fashion models are chosen because of their appeal to the young and vigorous. I suddenly discover a product that is essential, although I have been getting along without it all of my life. I disparage as outdated my perfectly serviceable possessions.

Heavenly Father, I pray that I will not allow advertisements to exploit my tendency to be discontented. Help me dismiss sales pitches that appeal to desire and pride. Keep me away from the idea that I can improve my future with things rather than by living for You.

RIGHTEOUSNESS

And the LORD said unto Noah, Come thou and all thy house into the ark; for thee have I seen righteous before me in this generation.
GENESIS 7:1

Lord, sometimes I look around and see all kinds of sin in this world. I let my guard down, and I am tempted to say or do something I know is wrong. In moments like that, I remember the account of Noah. He refused to compromise his righteous walk with You, Lord. The evil people of his day mocked him as he built the ark, but You honored his righteousness by saving him and his family from the Flood.

Dear God, help me to find favor in Your eyes by maintaining Christian traits. The most important concern in my life is to please You.

FATHER

*The father of the righteous shall
greatly rejoice: and he that begetteth
a wise child shall have joy of him.*
PROVERBS 23:24

Heavenly Father, I am perplexed by how the world sees fathers. In the old television shows, the man of the house was a wise, successful, and morally superior father. Today, the father is often portrayed as a bewildered but lovable buffoon who hasn't the foggiest notion of how to solve the problems his children face.

Father, I pray I can be like You in the essential points. Lead me to carry out the central duties of a father: providing care, love, protection, and guidance. Even when my children are not present, I desire my actions to be those of a godly father. Most important of all, I want to be the cornerstone of a righteous family.

THE REAL ARTICLE

But the wisdom that is from above is first pure, then peaceable, gentle, and easy to be intreated, full of mercy and good fruits, without partiality, and without hypocrisy.
JAMES 3:17

Father, years ago a coworker sold me a gold ring. After a hot and sweaty day, my skin under the ring had turned green. The ring was not pure gold but had only gold plating over copper.

Lord, I pray that my character is not a veneer on the outside. Instead, may the way that I appear on the outside flow from within. Through deliberate effort, I want to develop the attributes—honesty, honor, hospitality, and humility—from which character springs. Father, ensure that the words I say, the actions I take, and the thoughts of my heart are an indivisible combination that reflect a life dedicated to You.

TAKE WATER AND DRINK IT

But whosoever drinketh of the water that I shall give him shall never thirst; but the water that I shall give him shall be in him a well of water springing up into everlasting life.
JOHN 4:14

Heavenly Father, I saw a sign warning hikers going down into the Grand Canyon to take water and drink it. I was surprised at the second part of the warnings, but park rangers have found people unconscious from dehydration who were carrying full canteens. They had the water they needed to preserve their lives, but they failed to drink it.

Lord Jesus, I am blessed to have so many ways to learn about Your will. Yet, unless I make the effort to drink in Your Word, I am lost. The Bible says You, Lord Jesus, are the source of water that quenches spiritual thirst. Thank You for granting to me the water that brings life everlasting.

ON THE FRONT LINE

*And how shall they preach, except they be sent?
as it is written, How beautiful are the feet of them
that preach the gospel of peace, and bring
glad tidings of good things!*
ROMANS 10:15

Good Shepherd, I pray for the missionaries who teach the Gospel at the risk of their own lives. I cannot help but admire and support those brave individuals who are willing to follow that calling. May they radiate the Gospel by both their words and deeds to the destitute, sick, suffering, and spiritually barren.

Lord, may their example encourage me to support those who step out in faith so they will be fully equipped to effectively spread the Gospel to the world. Help them be full of energy. Protect them from those who resent their efforts.

BEYOND PETITION

Praying always with all prayer and supplication in the Spirit, and watching thereunto with all perseverance and supplication for all saints.
EPHESIANS 6:18

Father, although I pray with a submissive spirit, this matter is such a burden on my heart that it rises above a petition. I often pray from the intellect, without feeling emotion. My supplication this time is from a heart so burdened that I cannot find the words to express my needs.

I come before You in all humility and exhaustion. I am earnestly seeking Your mercy and compassion. Although things look bleak, I know You will show me a way through. Help me emerge on the other side with a stronger faith.

MINISTERS

And my speech and my preaching was not
with enticing words of man's wisdom, but in
demonstration of the Spirit and of power.
1 Corinthians 2:4

I come before You, Lord, asking that Your protection would be upon the ministers of the Gospel in this community. I ask You to raise up people with vision who can solve the difficulties of today and anticipate the problems of tomorrow. Help them have the wisdom to speak for You in love. Build a protective fence around them so they are left unscathed by those who belittle their efforts.

Father, I pray that I will do all I can to support those who bring Your Word to my community. May I stand with them so they have the courage to deliver Your message untainted by secular concerns.

HIDDEN WORKERS

And the eye cannot say unto the hand,
I have no need of thee: nor again the head
to the feet, I have no need of you.
1 Corinthians 12:21

Dear Lord, I'd planned to buy a pair of sneakers for outdoor walking. The sports store carried an array of choices: walking shoes, running shoes, rock-climbing shoes, cross-trainers, and sturdy hiking boots. Although I don't often think about my feet, the choices of footwear proved that they are as important as other parts of my body.

Father, remind me that those who work for You are all part of the body of Christ. As a Christian, I am often unaware of the importance of people who work behind the scenes, hidden because of their humility. Father, I pray that I will appreciate their efforts and tell them so. Guide me also to be a hidden servant.

INDIVIDUALS MATTER TO GOD

*So we, being many, are one body in Christ,
and every one members one of another.*
ROMANS 12:5

Lord, as a child I would stand over an anthill and watch ants go about their business. I marveled at their ceaseless effort. Yet, it bothered me that each worker ant was not clearly different from the others.

I rejoice that I have a unique personality. As a Christian, I have strengths and weaknesses. I have talents for some tasks but must depend upon others to carry out those jobs that I cannot do. I am Your gift to others—and they are Your gift to me. Dear God, help me use my individual abilities to share Your love with others.

VICTORY OVER SATAN

Submit yourselves therefore to God.
Resist the devil, and he will flee from you.
JAMES 4:7

Lord, my visits to the zoo always include a tour through the reptile house. The boa constrictor is big and strong. The poisonous rattlesnake provokes fear by the warning rattle of its tail. A walk by the snakes reminds me of the analogy of Satan to a serpent. But unlike reptiles, who avoid humans and strike only because they feel danger is near, Satan hunts victims to attack them.

Protective Lord, thank You for the promise that we can have victory over Satan by resisting him through Your name.

AGGRESSIVE FAITH

*I can do all things through Christ
which strengtheneth me.*
PHILIPPIANS 4:13

Father, I go out each day as a soldier for You. If I am rewarded with victory after victory, may I examine my goals in case I am aiming too low. Teach me to see clearly the battles You want me to fight. Give me the ability to think the impossible, and fill me with the aggressive faith to make it happen.

Battles are long and victories are short. I would rather enjoy victories than failure, but I would rather suffer a lost battle than stand on the sidelines and do nothing. Almighty God, I surrender myself to Your service.

HYPOCRISY

Let no man despise thy youth;
but be thou an example of the believers,
in word, in conversation, in charity,
in spirit, in faith, in purity.
1 TIMOTHY 4:12

Heavenly Father, I pray I never become a deceiver who tries to live two lives. Good cannot exist at the same time as deception. For if I live two lives, one of them must die. I pray that it is the false life, the hypocritical one that dies.

Lord, although I cannot achieve the sinless life of Christ, help me follow Your Word so closely that I illustrate a true Christian life. I pray that my example is not a poor copy but an original born in Your likeness, educated in Your love, and reflecting Your grandeur.

SPRING

*Then spake Jesus again unto them,
saying, I am the light of the world: he that
followeth me shall not walk in darkness,
but shall have the light of life.*
JOHN 8:12

Lord, spring is a time of growth and renewal, a time of new life, and a time of hope. This spring, an astonishing sight greeted me as I walked along a recently built walkway. A spring flower had managed to push through the hard asphalt. The delicate sprout had displayed unusual power as it shoved aside the material that blocked its way to sunlight.

Father, give me the determination to renew myself spiritually each day. I pray that I will have the strength of character to overcome those forces that are in the way of my growing in Your light.

GIVING OF MYSELF

And whosoever will be chief among you, let him
be your servant: even as the Son of man came
not to be ministered unto, but to minister,
and to give his life a ransom for many.
MATTHEW 20:27–28

As I contemplate all the activities that demand my attention, I think of You, Jesus. You did the work of a servant by washing the feet of the apostles. Please help me remember that the greatest in the kingdom of heaven is not the one being served, but the humble one doing the serving.

Sometimes I find it easier to give from a distance than to become personally involved in situations. Help me, Lord, to fulfill the mission to serve others. I need Your strength to meet my obligations to my family, my coworkers, and members of my community.

GUIDANCE

*For thou art my rock and my fortress;
therefore for thy name's sake
lead me, and guide me.*
PSALM 31:3

Lord, I sometimes look at every event as either a positive or negative, an advance toward a goal or a detour away from it. I wonder why a promotion did not occur or why, if it did, it had unforeseen negative consequences.

Dear Lord, let me never become so determined to reach my goal that I fail to see Your hand guiding my life in the plan that You have set for me. May I continue to set short-term goals and make long-range plans but temper my expectations with thought and prayer.

THE THIRD ROAD

Open to me the gates of righteousness: I will go into them, and I will praise the Lord: this gate of the Lord, into which the righteous shall enter.
PSALM 118:19–20

Heavenly Father, I read in Your Word about two roads—one to destruction and one to eternal life. In my ignorance, I seek a third road built especially for me. It's a comfortable way—one that accommodates an agreeable husband, dutiful father, dependable employee, and occasional community volunteer. It requires only halfhearted service to You without the full acceptance of the blood of Jesus.

Lord, I do realize that there are two roads, not three. The road I take depends on the gate that I walk through. Lord, guide me through the gate that leads to eternal life.

MATERIAL WEALTH

Let your conversation be without covetousness; and be content with such things as ye have: for he hath said, I will never leave thee, nor forsake thee.
HEBREWS 13:5

Dear Lord, You know I worry about money. Not because I am afraid I will not have enough, but because of my concern for those who depend upon me. I feel a strong obligation to provide for my family.

Lord, prevent me from using my role as a provider to rationalize an excessive devotion to making money. I pray that I will never measure success by material wealth or possessions or think of money as a symbol of my virility. Thank You for assuring me that You will provide for my needs.

ETERNAL LIFE

In my Father's house are many mansions:
if it were not so, I would have told you.
I go to prepare a place for you.
JOHN 14:2

Lord, as I walk through the house in the mornings, especially on cold days, I feel the onset of middle age. I have aches in my back and pains in my joints. A look in the mirror assures me that evolution is not at work. Rather than becoming a higher order, my body is falling into disarray.

Lord, I realize You have numbered my days on this earth for a good reason. You have prepared for me an everlasting home with You in heaven. Thank You, Lord, for the promise of eternal life. I can face the future with hope.

FILLING UP WITH POWER

Strengthened with all might, according to his glorious power, unto all patience and longsuffering with joyfulness.
COLOSSIANS 1:11

Father, I watch with admiration as speedway pit crews service racecars. Drivers try to come in under a caution flag, but if there is no caution, they come in anyway for fuel, a change of tires, and minor repairs. They understand that even in the most tightly contested race, they must have regular pit stops.

Dear Lord, teach me to take the necessary breaks that give You time to make repairs in my heart and mind. When I fail to read the Bible and talk to You, my spiritual life runs low on power. In the race to heaven, keep me tuned up and filled with the faith I need to successfully finish my course.

EYES FORWARD

I will lift up mine eyes unto the hills, from whence cometh my help. My help cometh from the Lord, which made heaven and earth.
PSALM 121:1–2

Father, I become distracted by events that take place around me. But when I turn my eyes toward You, I can see that enduring the trials of this life are well worth where You are taking me.

Sometimes my prayers are filled with concerns. I come with intercession for others, a petition for my own needs, and an entreaty for forgiveness. Build in me the assurance that You are sympathetic toward the matters that I bring before You. I know that comfort is only a prayer away. Thank You for listening to my appeal.

A LIVING STONE

Ye also, as lively stones, are built up a
spiritual house, an holy priesthood,
to offer up spiritual sacrifices,
acceptable to God by Jesus Christ.
1 PETER 2:5

Lord, I am amazed at the ceaseless action of waves. I find stones that are rounded smooth by the continuous pounding of the water. Even the edges of broken glass are smoothed away until they are no longer sharp.

Father, I see Your ceaseless action on my life in the same way. Day by day, You remove my rough edges. You blunt my sharp tongue, soften my overbearing manner, cool my hot temper, and smooth out my uneven disposition. From a rough and unremarkable stone, You have made me into something better. Thank You for continuously changing me.

FOR UNITY
OF BELIEVERS

And the glory which thou gavest me I have given them; that they may be one, even as we are one.
JOHN 17:22

Righteous Father, I am humbled when I realize that Jesus, on the night He was betrayed, prayed for the unity of believers. I look at Your Word through different eyes than other Christians and often cannot fully agree with them. Help me focus on our many vital common beliefs rather than our few trivial differences. Help me see the strength in unity and the danger of discord.

Often it is easy to agree if the agreement is to do nothing. Let my agreement be to act and do, not sit back and wait. Let me join the fellowship of believers so we become a force for righteousness.

CORROSION RESISTANT

*Woe unto you, scribes and Pharisees,
hypocrites! for ye are like unto whited
sepulchres, which indeed appear beautiful
outward, but are within full of dead
men's bones, and of all uncleanness.*
MATTHEW 23:27

Dear Lord, I can tell when iron becomes rusty because the color of the rust is different from the color of the metal. I understand, however, that some metals have rust that is the same color as the underlying metal. The metal continues to weaken, yet there is no outward sign of the problem.

Jesus, I pray that You will come to my rescue when sin attacks me. Open my eyes so that I will see my transgressions and avoid them in the future. Lord, guard me from the sin that can reach below the surface. Keep my life free from corruption.

AT MEALTIME

And God said, Behold, I have given you every
herb bearing seed, which is upon the face of all
the earth, and every tree, in the which is the fruit
of a tree yielding seed; to you it shall be for meat.
GENESIS 1:29

I praise You, living God, who made all things. You spoke into existence the plant and animal kingdoms. You created a people in Your image to take care of Your creation.

Thank You, Lord, for the fruitful seasons that are made possible by Your design—the seasons of seedtime and harvest. I see eternity in the seeds of each fruit and vegetable because they ensure a harvest year after year. For the blessings of the dinner table, whether a simple staple like bread or a hearty main course, I give You praise, O Lord.

IN THE MORNING

This is the day which the Lord hath made;
we will rejoice and be glad in it.
PSALM 118:24

Good morning, Lord. As my first talk with You today, I want to thank You for giving me another day. I don't know what it holds, but I am thankful that I have another opportunity to live for You.

Later I'll bring to You those specific needs that arise each day. I will speak the names of people who need Your special touch. Now, however, I give You thanks and I praise You. More than anything else, I want to acknowledge who You are and not just what You have done. You are the reason I get up each morning.

IN THE EVENING

Let my prayer be set forth before thee
as incense; and the lifting up of my
hands as the evening sacrifice.
PSALM 141:2

Lord, I have seen relationships dissolve because of a failure to communicate. The lack of an interchange of thoughts and information caused erosion in the friendly camaraderie.

I ask that You will help me to relate well with my family and associates. On a spiritual level, I pray that my heavenly communication keeps a clear line of sending and receiving messages from You. In this evening prayer, I want to evaluate my relationship with You. Staying in contact with You, Lord, has the eternal importance of helping me realize my blessings and translating them into actions to share with others.

CONFESSION

Whosoever shall confess
that Jesus is the Son of God,
God dwelleth in him, and he in God.
1 JOHN 4:15

Father, I confess that my life is not all that it should be. Even by my own standards, I fall far below what I want to accomplish. I can never be a perfect Christian, and my distress becomes even greater when I compare myself to Jesus.

Dear Savior, my heart rejoices because my life becomes acceptable to You when I put on the cloak of Jesus. He brings me to all righteousness. I will confess my sins, renew myself in You, and set out again refreshed, determined to do better.

DRIVING ON HIGH BEAM

Let your light so shine before men, that they may see your good works, and glorify your Father which is in heaven.
MATTHEW 5:16

Father, when I am driving in the country late at night, I am thankful to have the brilliant high-beam headlights to warn me of deer that might wander onto the road. The focused, concentrated light gives me advance warning of any dangers ahead of me.

Dear Jesus, You gave Your disciples the responsibility of living as lights to guide the lost to You. Let Your heavenly beams shine through my life to reveal You as the Savior of the world and to focus praise on the Father. Help me to be diligent in illuminating the narrow road that leads to heaven.

NEW LIFE

*A good man leaveth an inheritance
to his children's children.*
PROVERBS 13:22

Eight pounds and eight ounces, twenty-one inches long. Father, as I hold my newborn son and watch him sleep in peace, I cannot help but wonder what the future holds. A lot is expected of me—and of him. He will carry my name and represent me by extending my hopes beyond what I have accomplished.

Dear Lord, I pray I will give him the freedom to find his own way but also ground him in the essentials of Your Word. I pray that he will inherit from me a name that he will be pleased to wear. But more than anything, I pray that I will see his name written beside mine in the Book of Life.

KEEPING IN TUNE

For it had been better for them not to have known the way of righteousness, than, after they have known it, to turn from the holy commandment delivered unto them.
2 PETER 2:21

Father, while visiting a pioneer village with my children, we watched a blacksmith making horseshoes. He held the iron bar on the anvil as his other arm swung the heavy hammer. To shape the horseshoe, he moved the iron but kept the hammer going at a steady pace, as if playing a tune. He could work for hours without getting tired because he let the hammer have its way.

Father, help me recognize the advantages of keeping in tune with Your decrees. Many of my problems come from trying to bend Your will to my goals. Instead, help me work with You rather than against You.

THE MASTER'S VOICE

But be ye doers of the word, and not hearers only,
deceiving your own selves.
JAMES 1:22

Dear Lord, I am thankful that You were kind enough to provide Your Word. The orderliness of nature tells me of Your existence; I would be miserable knowing that You had created me but then abandoned Your creation. I sense Your presence when I read the Bible. I hear Your voice and learn that You take a personal interest in me. Your Word gives me a glimpse of You.

Lord, I pray for the will to read Your Word, a mind to understand its meaning, the ability to apply its principles to my life, and the determination to act upon what I learn.

VIEW FROM A HEIGHT

*For the eyes of the Lord are over the righteous,
and his ears are open unto their prayers.*
1 Peter 3:12

Dear Lord, viewing the world from a thousand feet above it in a hot air balloon gives me an unusual perspective. I can see a canoe that will hit rapids around the bend in the stream. I see cars coming toward one another along a country lane, but because of a hill, the drivers can't see each other. My eyes are no sharper than theirs, but I can see objects hidden from them because I have a different vantage point.

Father, I know You have a better viewpoint. You can see into my heart and into my future. You can see what is coming and prepare me for it. Please continue to watch over me.

REFRESHMENT

Restore unto me the joy of thy salvation;
and uphold me with thy free spirit.
PSALM 51:12

Father, as a young boy on a farm, I viewed rainy days with pleasure. My outdoor chores were put aside, and I could devote a few hours of time to my special interests. Afterward, I would return to my chores with renewed vigor. As an adult, I sometimes view rain with less enjoyment. I become exasperated if I must change my plans. But even as I find rain an unwelcome inconvenience, I recognize it as an essential part of nature.

Heavenly Father, help me recognize that the difficulties in my life are like rain. The interruptions to my routine give me opportunities to refresh my spirit.

DESTROYING DARKNESS

*For the commandment is a lamp;
and the law is light; and reproofs of
instruction are the way of life.*
PROVERBS 6:23

Dear Father, every time I replace a lightbulb, I wonder why it burned out so quickly. Regardless of its limits, I am thankful for light that expels darkness.

Lord, because You used the example of light throughout scripture, I am able to understand Your holy character and comprehend the power that You have to destroy the darkness of sin. Jesus, let Your light shine through me so others will be exposed to the heavenly light that You delivered to earth long ago. I pray for Your guidance in my effort to share Your light with the lost world.

VOTING WITH MY WALLET

For we are his workmanship, created in Christ Jesus unto good works, which God hath before ordained that we should walk in them.
EPHESIANS 2:10

Lord, thank You for the freedom I have to vote for candidates and issues both on the local and national level. I pray for Your guidance in carrying out this responsibility.

Similarly, Lord, I will express my convictions about spiritual issues by the choices I make. Help me be responsible in the causes that I choose to support. Guide me in the purchases I make, the businesses I patronize, and the entertainment venues I attend. Heavenly Father, let every vote I cast, either at the polls or with my wallet, make this country a more righteous nation.

SACRIFICE OF PRAISE

*By him therefore let us offer the sacrifice of
praise to God continually, that is, the fruit
of our lips giving thanks to his name.*
HEBREWS 13:15

Lord, my life has been relatively devoid of the kinds
of sacrifices made by Christian pioneers of the past.
What sacrifices can I make?

Heavenly Father, I sacrifice to You my self-will.
To the one and only living God, I submit my life as an
offering of worship. Another sacrifice I offer is one
of praise. Purify my mouth that my praise may be
acceptable to You. I give thanks for Your redemption.
All praise, honor, and glory belong to You.

REVIVE ME

Nevertheless I have somewhat against thee, because thou hast left thy first love. Remember therefore from whence thou art fallen, and repent, and do the first works.
REVELATION 2:4–5

Father, I sometimes become so captivated by the concerns of my daily life that I lose interest in my spiritual life. I struggle through a morass of uncon-cern for others and even for myself. I forget my calling as Your child.

Lord, I acknowledge my apathy and ignorance and realize that my lassitude comes from a lack of drinking from Your refreshing water. I need to renew myself with prayer, study Your Word, and fellowship with other Christians. Give me new momentum. Revitalize my life. Restore the intensity of my first love for You.

COMFORT OF
THE HOLY SPIRIT

*But the Comforter. . .shall teach you all things,
and bring all things to your remembrance,
whatsoever I have said unto you.*
JOHN 14:26

Lord Jesus, just before You ascended into heaven, the disciples wondered what would happen to them after You went away. You told them that You would send the Holy Spirit to be their comforter and teacher. By Your power they were able to boldly spread the Good News throughout the sinful world.

Today, Lord, I want to thank You for the gift of the Spirit working through Your children. I trust Your power to give me joy and hope. Produce spiritual fruit in my life and pour Your love in my heart by the Holy Spirit.

PROTECTION OF JESUS

The God of my rock; in him will I trust:
he is my shield, and the horn of my salvation,
my high tower, and my refuge, my saviour;
thou savest me from violence.
2 Samuel 22:3

Dear Lord, as a young child, my walk home from a friend's house took me through a small patch of woods. This particular grove always appeared exceptionally dark. The moist earth around the roots carried an unpleasant dank smell. I would pull my coat around me and hurry by while I tried to act braver than I actually felt.

Jesus, I'm traveling through Satan's realm. Although this world is not my final destination, I must pass through it on my way home. I pray for You to cover me and surround me with Your atoning blood. With Your robe of righteousness, Satan cannot harm me.

HEAVENLY ROAD MAP

*Come unto me, all ye that labour and are
heavy laden, and I will give you rest.*
MATTHEW 11:28

Lord, I plan a driving trip in exhaustive detail, high-lighting the best route on the map, pinning down stopovers, and identifying points of interest. All of this requires a great deal of study that begins weeks before the departure date.

Father, I pray that I might take far more care in planning my trip to heaven. I don't know how much time I have to prepare for it, but while there is still time, I will talk to You in prayer, study the Bible to learn Your will, and work to be a faithful servant. Write on my heart the heavenly road map.

SUPPLICATION

Be careful for nothing; but in every thing by prayer and supplication with thanksgiving let your requests be made known unto God.
PHILIPPIANS 4:6

Father, I am aware of many people who are suffering and who are in difficult situations. I pray that they and their families will be able to work out the difficulty. Help me to find a way to ease their burden.

I pray also for those people who live lives of quiet desperation—those who never reveal their distress but suffer in silent hopelessness. I pray that I will be sensitive to these individuals, recognize their concerns, and take action to relieve them of the suffering they are trying to bear by themselves.

TELL OTHERS
ABOUT JESUS

Now then we are ambassadors for Christ.
2 CORINTHIANS 5:20

Lord, I made a great purchase the other day. The price was right, the quality was exceptional, and it fitted my needs perfectly. At least two of my friends decided to take my advice and buy the same product.

Lord, I understand that the Good News of Jesus is vastly more important than a shopping special. You have made the greatest difference in my life. I must speak to others about what You have done for me. I want to be a persuasive representative for You to my family and friends. Direct my speech so I can effectively convey to them how Jesus can change their lives too.

ILLUMINATE BUT DON'T BLIND

Ye are all the children of light, and the children of the day: we are not of the night, nor of darkness.
1 Thessalonians 5:5

Lord, the other night during a power failure, I was the first to find a flashlight. The little light was enough to dispel the darkness. Because I carried the light, my family members gathered around me.

Your radiance illuminates all creation, yet I see people stumbling in spiritual gloom. Although I am but a pale reflection of Your brilliance, I pray that my teaching will become a beacon that draws lost souls into the circle of Your light. May my light never dazzle but rather reveal. Guide me so that I push out the darkness and fill others' lives with the light of Christ.

PAGES OF TIME

Let not mercy and truth forsake thee:
bind them about thy neck; write them
upon the table of thine heart.
PROVERBS 3:3

Lord, with my smartphone, I can specify the subjects that are displayed on my screen. I can choose the news content, weather report, financial statements, sports scores, and entertainment guide. I can personalize it to my taste.

Father, today You have given me a fresh page of my life. I can write upon it words that encourage or words that destroy, acts of kindness or selfish deeds, thoughts that cause my spirit to soar or ideas that bring me low. Let me wisely choose the content of my life to glorify You.

TRUST IN HIS DEFENSE

But let all those that put their trust in thee rejoice:
let them ever shout for joy, because thou
defendest them: let them also that love
thy name be joyful in thee.
PSALM 5:11

Thankfully, dear Jesus, I have never been falsely accused of a crime and had to stand trial. Should that unfortunate event occur, I would want a skilled defense attorney to plead my case and believable witnesses to establish my innocence.

Lord, the Bible says that You defend those who believe in You. When Satan brings charges against my life or character, I am encouraged that You are my defense attorney and also my witness. Thank You for accepting my faith and trust as the evidence You need to render the verdict "Not guilty! Case closed!"

EQUAL IN HONOR

Honour all men. Love the brotherhood.
Fear God. Honour the king.
1 PETER 2:17

Father, You have made me a unique individual. You have bestowed upon me a unique dignity. I may gain wealth or descend into poverty, become well-known or live in obscurity, receive prestige or be ignored. Regardless of those circumstances, I am equal in honor with everyone else because I am made in Your image.

Remind me, O Lord, that the truth of equal honor applies to others I meet. May I treat them with dignity and respect and see Your likeness in them.

VICTORY OVER THE GIANT

*David said moreover, The LORD that delivered
me out of the paw of the lion, and out of
the paw of the bear, he will deliver me
out of the hand of this Philistine.*
1 SAMUEL 17:37

Dear God, I work out in a gym, but despite my efforts,
I will probably never be as strong as some of the
men there who lift weights.

Mighty Lord, I am happy that You do not require
physical strength to do battle for righteousness.
You helped young David defeat Goliath with just
one stone and a sling because he trusted You to be
his deliverer. Likewise, I offer You my faith with the
understanding that You will make it powerful enough
to conquer situations regardless of how hopeless
they may seem.

CLOTHED IN RIGHTEOUSNESS

Because thou sayest, I am rich, and increased with goods, and have need of nothing; and knowest not that thou art wretched, and miserable, and poor, and blind, and naked.
REVELATION 3:17

Heavenly Father, although I do not think of myself as rich, I have always had a home, food, and clothing. I recognize my happy circumstances when I think of those prophets of old who had stones for their pillows.

More importantly are the spiritual riches You give me. At one time I was walking in darkness, starved for love and unprotected from Satan. Now I am sheltered in Your love, nourished by Your Word, and clothed in the protection of the Holy Spirit. I love You, Lord, and will always be mindful of the rich blessings that fall on me.

DANGEROUSLY DEAD

Trust ye in the Lord for ever: for in the Lord Jehovah is everlasting strength.
ISAIAH 26:4

Lord, the great oak tree had become dangerously dead, but no one could tell. The death was in the heartwood, working from the inside out. When the storm came, the trunk snapped, fell, and crushed some smaller trees nearby.

Father, sometimes I become enamored with people that I consider towering Christians. But I cannot see their hearts, and occasionally their lives collapse because they have become only a shell of Christianity. When they fall, I become disillusioned. Father, I pray that Satan does not destroy those individuals who are in the public eye. I pray also that my trust will always be in You as my unfailing leader.

THE GENUINE ARTICLE

Whatsoever things are true, whatsoever things are honest, whatsoever things are just, whatsoever things are pure, whatsoever things are lovely, whatsoever things are of good report. . .think on these things.
PHILIPPIANS 4:8

Father, I can see in my daily activities how people strive for simple perfection: a mathematical proof that solves a problem in the least number of steps, a musical composition without a discordant note, a work of art that achieves harmony and symmetric composition.

Dear Lord, I strive for a life in tune with Your orchestration. I know that to have an honorable life, I must be meticulous in eliminating the inferior elements and strive to reflect Your higher nature. I want to be a genuine Christian. I put my life in Your hands so that I can come closer to reaching that goal.

INDEPENDENCE DAY

And ye shall know the truth,
and the truth shall make you free.
JOHN 8:32

Heavenly Father, summer travel brochures always seem to show a person strolling along a white sandy beach, lying in a hammock, or watching a sunset. My vacations aren't as leisure filled, and by the time they are over, I look forward to returning to work. Independence Day is my favorite summer holiday because it lasts only one day—a backyard barbecue, a ball game, evening fireworks, and it is over.

Thank You, Lord, for my personal independence day, the day You broke me away from sin so I could begin a personal, daily association with You as my guide.

RICHES FROM HEAVEN

Charge them that are rich in this world,
that they be not highminded, nor trust in
uncertain riches, but in the living God,
who giveth us richly all things to enjoy.
1 Timothy 6:17

Almighty Father of all creation, I look around and see the good things You have provided. I realize everything comes from You, even my ability to earn a living. When I give back my small offering and reflect on the blessings that You have given me, I cannot help but say, "Thank You, Lord, for letting me use the rest."

Yes, Lord, I understand that the congregation requires this voluntary contribution for its Christian activities in my community. I give it for that purpose in part, but more importantly, I use it to express my gratitude for the spiritual and material blessings I enjoy every day.

READ THE DIRECTIONS

*All scripture is given by inspiration of God,
and is profitable for doctrine, for reproof,
for correction, for instruction in righteousness:
that the man of God may be perfect,
thoroughly furnished unto all good works.*
2 TIMOTHY 3:16–17

Father, I spent a morning trying to put together the barbecue grill, which was labeled SOME ASSEMBLY REQUIRED. If I had read the directions to begin with, it would have been simpler. Maybe. Even when I did bring myself to read the instructions, I couldn't figure out what was required of me.

Sometimes, Lord, I try to put my life together without reading the directions. Emotions and feelings cannot be trusted to lead me in the right direction. Thank You for providing a clear set of directions for my life. Thankfully, I can read Your Word and understand the principles that make me—Your creation—function correctly.

CREATIVE EFFORT

A faithful man shall abound with blessings:
but he that maketh haste to be
rich shall not be innocent.
PROVERBS 28:20

Father, I must take prudent risks in my business and personal life. I must be willing to enter new ventures even if success is not certain. However, I should not participate in risky ventures such as gambling. Convenience stores and other outlets sell lottery tickets, and across the country are glitzy casinos.

Help me recognize them for what they are—get-rich-quick schemes that rely on luck rather than You. Help me build my life on creative efforts and useful skills. Prevent me from being enticed into a gambler's way of thinking.

TRUST IN HIS RIGHTEOUSNESS

In thee, O Lord, do I put my trust; let me never be ashamed: deliver me in thy righteousness.
PSALM 31:1

Heavenly Father, I look at a photo of myself taken years ago and marvel at how much I have changed. The greatest change has been on the inside. Righteous Lord, before I made a commitment to You, I tried to run my own life. I ignored the advice of friends and became angry over their concern for me. My emotions were out of control. Today, I wonder how anyone managed to tolerate me.

Thank You, Lord, for delivering me from my former self. No longer do I feel I must be a self-made man. I experience peace in knowing You as my Savior. I trust You to be my guide.

A TOOL FOR EVERY TASK

*I therefore, the prisoner of the Lord,
beseech you that ye walk worthy of the
vocation wherewith ye are called.*
EPHESIANS 4:1

Father, I am impressed when I watch a skilled carpenter or auto mechanic at work. I am struck by how they select a tool that is perfectly fitted for the task at hand.

Dear Lord, I see that You have given me particular skills and abilities. Others can fill in for me when I do not do the jobs for which I have been created. However, You have called me into service to apply my unique talents to those tasks that I do best. May I never evade my responsibilities by claiming that someone else is better qualified.

TEACHING ABOUT JESUS

These are the things that ye shall do; Speak ye every man the truth to his neighbour; execute the judgment of truth and peace in your gates.
ZECHARIAH 8:16

Lord Jesus, I occasionally take on the role of teacher, although I often feel inadequate for the task. My goal is to be a mentor, guide, and advisor. May I grow in knowledge, wisdom, character, and confidence so I can help those I teach to choose the proper path.

Heavenly Teacher, provide me with the ability to instill in my students a love for learning more about You, reading the Bible, talking to You in prayer, and living a life in keeping with Your Word. May I have an influence that will last a lifetime.

GRACIOUS GIFT

*For all things are for your sakes, that the
abundant grace might through the thanksgiving
of many redound to the glory of God.*
2 CORINTHIANS 4:15

Father, I express to You my thanksgiving for all that
You provide. I know that all good things come from
You. It is not by my hands or my ability but by Your
gracious gifts that I am able to earn a living and
provide for my family.

Dear Provider, as I employ the skills You have
given me to accomplish my duties in the workday
world, so I pray that I will employ my talents in the
spiritual world. I pray that I will use my talents to
show Your love to others.

MORE LIKE YOU

That they all may be one; as thou, Father, art in me, and I in thee, that they also may be one in us: that the world may believe that thou hast sent me.
JOHN 17:21

Father, when I see an elderly couple that has spent a lifetime together in love, I find it remarkable how they anticipate one another's needs, how they communicate with merely a nod or a gesture, and, in some cases, how they have developed similar physical characteristics.

Father, I pray that during my life, I can in the same way become one with You. I want to absorb Your Word so thoroughly that I know Your will because it has become a part of me. I pray that I can talk with You easily and often because it has become my nature. And most of all, I pray that I will have the same spiritual characteristics as You.

MONEY MATTERS

For the love of money is the root of all evil:
which while some coveted after, they have erred
from the faith, and pierced themselves
through with many sorrows.
1 TIMOTHY 6:10

Lord, deliver me from coveting the riches of this world. Protect me from the evils that are associated with wanting inordinate wealth. May I never compromise my service to You by mistakenly thinking I can protect my future through a healthy bank account.

Father God, I do desire health and prosperity, but You are a good shepherd, and through You I am led to eternal blessings. Help me keep my faith grounded in You so that my mind and heart will not be overtaken with greed. May I stay aware of Satan's tactics to turn blessings into reproach. Give me wisdom to be a trusting steward.

BLESS MY DEEDS

*But whoso looketh into the perfect law of liberty,
and continueth therein, he being not a forgetful
hearer, but a doer of the work, this man
shall be blessed in his deed.*
JAMES 1:25

Father, I like to play football from the comfort of my living room. From my safe haven on the couch, I yell at players for making mistakes and criticize the coach's decisions. A crossing pattern here, a quarterback sneak there. If I were a coach, what magnificent plays I would call!

Lord, in church projects I often contribute more advice than work. It is so much easier to tell a person what needs to be done than to actually do it. Help me to get involved in church business. Give me a spirit of unity and a positive attitude in working with others to build up Your kingdom. Thank You for promising to bless my deeds.

VITAL GIVING

*The thoughts of the diligent tend only to
plenteousness; but of every one that
is hasty only to want.*
PROVERBS 21:5

Lord, it seems every cause has a compelling reason for me to support its effort. I find it difficult to separate the vital few from the trivial many. I cannot learn enough about every group's programs to fully support what they are doing. Give me the wisdom to direct my support to those who are carrying out Your will. I pray I will always be willing to make sacrifices, but keep me from being a wasteful giver.

Heavenly Father, guide me to practical ways that I can support those who are doing Your will.

A GIFT FROM GOD

Give, and it shall be given unto you. . . .
For with the same measure that ye mete
withal it shall be measured to you again.
LUKE 6:38

Lord, You set the standard for generosity by giving up Your life for a sinful world. May I always be reminded of Your sacrifice when I see a need that I can fill. Just as a farmer plants seeds and profits from the harvest, You also bless those who share their assets.

Heavenly Father, help me to give out of a pure motive to bless those in need, not out of a selfish expectation of reward. I truly want to act as Your hand extended to help those who have physical, spiritual, and financial needs.

GREET THEM WITH A SMILE

*But straightway Jesus spake unto them, saying,
Be of good cheer; it is I; be not afraid.*
MATTHEW 14:27

Dear Jesus, just as You told Your followers to be of good cheer, may I recognize that You want me to heed those words as well. My experience confirms what scientific research has shown—a cheerful personality can overcome physical and mental afflictions. A positive attitude allows the body to heal.

Lord, give me a cheerful disposition, not only to benefit myself but also to bless others. I know that a good attitude can be a great influence for You. Help my joy spread to all those I meet.

UPRIGHTNESS

He kneeled upon his knees three times a day,
and prayed, and gave thanks before
his God, as he did aforetime.
DANIEL 6:10

Lord, I want to live an upright life no matter how difficult the circumstances. I look to Daniel as an example of one who was not afraid to do what was right, even though he faced death in a den of lions. You gave him protection and blessed his integrity.

When I face tough times, I pray I will continue to put my trust in You, O Lord. Give me a strong faith like Daniel's. You are more powerful than any enemies of my soul, and You have every situation in my life under control.

A CLEAR CONSCIENCE

*Pray for us: for we trust we have a good
conscience, in all things willing to live honestly.*
HEBREWS 13:18

Father, at the end of each day my mind replays the day's activities. I ask myself whether the decisions I made were the correct ones: Was I honest in my business transactions? Did I uphold a standard of integrity? Many judgments I made had to be made quickly, without much time for consideration.

Almighty Father, I pray that the pure thoughts and values taught in Your Word will direct my mind. I want to have the peace of a clear conscience as I go to sleep at night.

PANIC

And he said unto me, My grace is sufficient for thee: for my strength is made perfect in weakness.
2 Corinthians 12:9

Dear Lord, when evil unleashes its destructive forces, I feel overwhelmed. Whether it is an unexpected financial upheaval, a change in work assignment, an unfavorable doctor's report, or a personal crisis, panic bubbles below the surface. Dread hovers over me like an oppressive cloud and dampens my spirit. Fear and doubt create havoc in my otherwise rational mind.

Because panic becomes contagious and sets off a frenzy around me, I must not give in to panic. I pray for You to silence the alarms in my life. Teach me to be composed in the midst of uncertainty.

EMERGENCY RESPONSE

The LORD is my shepherd; I shall not want.
He maketh me to lie down in green pastures:
he leadeth me beside the still waters.
He restoreth my soul.
PSALM 23:1–3

Father, the feeling of foreboding was upon me again. I knew that something awful was going to happen. So I came to You in prayer and read the Psalms. That time of meditation cleared the mental overcast. I saw that the day was bright and sunny, and the disasters I had imagined never occurred.

Father, help me keep the well of anxiety empty. Prevent me from refilling it by brooding over past events or imagining future disasters. Help me face the issues that cause my anxiety and build my response upon realistic assumptions. I will stay in touch with You so that I may look to the future with hope.

LOVE

Know therefore that the L<small>ORD</small> thy God, he is God, the faithful God, which keepeth covenant and mercy with them that love him and keep his commandments to a thousand generations.
D<small>EUTERONOMY</small> 7:9

Omnipotent Father, there are no limitations to the amount of love and attention You can bestow upon each of Your children. Although I receive Your rich blessings all the time, day and night, I pray that I will not take Your love for granted.

Lord, the more I know You and understand You, the more I will see and appreciate Your love. I pray that I will experience You more deeply so that my love for You will increase. You have taught me that sacrifices must be made for love to grow. I submit to You. Demolish me and then rebuild me so I may be one with You.

FORGIVING OTHERS

*For thou, Lord, art good, and ready
to forgive; and plenteous in mercy
unto all them that call upon thee.*
PSALM 86:5

Lord, it is easy to justify my own mistakes. Yet, I find it difficult to cut any slack for others. When I am late to a meeting, I think it is for a good reason. When others are late, I think it is because of their incompetence or lack of commitment to their responsibilities.

Lord, that is the way my thinking often goes, and I know it is not right. Help me to stop accusing others while excusing my own shortcomings. With Your help, I will show others the same tolerance You have shown me. By forgiving others, I accept Your free grace.

SCRIPTURE INDEX